The
Wadsworth
Handbook
Workbook

The Wadsworth Handbook

Workbook

Eighth Edition

Kirszner & Mandell

Prepared by
Roxanne F. Munch
Joliet Junior College

THOMSON

WADSWORTH

Australia   Brazil   Canada   Mexico   Singapore   Spain   United Kingdom   United States

The Wadsworth Handbook Workbook
Eighth Edition
Roxanne F. Munch

Publisher: *Lyn Uhl*
Senior Acquisitions Editor: *Star MacKenzie Burruto*
Assistant Editor: *Cheryl Forman*
Senior Content Project Manager: *Lianne Ames*
Associate Content Project Manager: *Jessica Rasile*
Technology Project Manager: *Stephanie Gregoire*
Production Service/Compositor: *Nesbitt Graphics Inc.*
Senior Print Buyer: *Mary Beth Hennebury*
Text & Cover Printer: *Thomson West*

Printed in the United States of America
1 2 3 4 5 6   12 11 10 09 08 07

Thomson Higher Education
25 Thomson Place
Boston, MA 02210-1202
USA

For more information about our products, contact us at:
Thomson Learning
Academic Resource Center
1-800-423-0563

For permission to use material from this text or product, submit a request online at **http://www.thomsonrights.com**

Any additional questions about permissions can be submitted by e-mail to
thomsonrights@thomson.com

ISBN-13: 978-1-4130-3270-3
ISBN-10: 1-4130-3270-2

Contents

Chapter 1 Understanding Purpose, Audience, and Tone

Exercise A   1a Determining Your Purpose

Read the following four paragraphs. They are essentially on the same topic, the U.S.S. *Arizona* Memorial and Pearl Harbor. Identify the purpose of each passage. Then, select a place you have visited and write at least two paragraphs on the place using two purposes.

PARAGRAPH A

The haunting beauty of the U.S.S. *Arizona* Memorial, which seems to float on the clear blue waters of Pearl Harbor in Hawaii, is a perfect testimony to the tragedy that took place on December 7, 1941. Visitors linger over the names inscribed in the white marble, respectfully whispering. Some search for names, and others search the waters, staring at the rusting remains of the battleship U.S.S. *Arizona*. As the National Park Service Web site reminds us, this national shrine "symbolizes American sacrifice and resolve." A visit to this shrine is a reminder of lives lost, of young men whose futures were canceled but whose sacrifice will not be forgotten.

Purpose: _____

_____

_____

_____

_____

_____

_____

_____

_____

_____

PARAGRAPH B

The U.S.S. *Arizona* Memorial is the final resting place of the 1,177 men who lost their lives on December 7, 1941. The structure is 184 feet long and spans the midportion of the sunken battleship. The memorial consists of three parts: the entry and assembly rooms, a central area for observation and ceremonies, and a shrine room where the names of those killed are engraved on the marble wall. Creation of the memorial was approved by President Dwight D. Eisenhower in 1958, and construction was completed in 1961. It was funded through private donations and public funds appropriated by Congress. Visitor information and photographs may be accessed at the Web site for the National Park Service at www.nps.gov/usar/.

Purpose: _____

_____

_____

_____

_____

_____

_____

_____

_____

PARAGRAPH C

Could the American military have prevented the devastation that took place at Pearl Harbor on December 7, 1941? By 1941, Japan had joined the Axis Alliance with Nazi Germany, and the United States had applied pressures on Japan, including an oil embargo. While Japan's goals of conquest of the Western Pacific were becoming evident, the United States had located most of its Pacific Fleet in Pearl Harbor. Seven of the Fleet's nine battleships were moored along "Battleship Row"; naval aircraft were congregated nearby; and aircraft were parked in groups at Hickam, Wheeler, and Bellows airfields.

The attack came as a complete surprise; perhaps a better strategy in locating equipment and personnel could have saved lives and resources.

Purpose: _____

_____

_____

_____

_____

_____

_____

_____

_____

_____

PARAGRAPH D

The competition for an appropriate memorial for the World Trade Center, where so many lost their lives on September 11, 2001, has led to extensive controversy. Perhaps an examination of the U.S.S. *Arizona* Memorial in Honolulu, Hawaii, and the Vietnam Memorial in Washington, DC, can provide some insight into creating enduring monuments with aesthetic appeal. Both works are stark in their simplicity, yet both appeal visually. The graceful curve of the white marble monument that seems to float above Pearl Harbor suggests serenity. The bold wall of polished black marble inscribed with the names of those who died in Vietnam rises gradually above the viewer as the walkway slopes downward. Visitors cannot help but sense the magnitude of the war and the loss of young lives. A monument to the people who died on 9/11 should inspire the same awe and respect.

Purpose: _____

_____

_____

Chapter 1   Understanding Purpose, Audience, and Tone

Exercise B   1c Setting Your Tone

Paragraph A from Exercise A: 1a is repeated below. It is then revised to alter the tone. Read each paragraph and do the following:

1. Discuss the tone of each passage.
2. Identify the key words and phrases that affect the tone.
3. Attempt to rewrite it to achieve another tone.
4. Discuss reasons for the changes made.
5. Even though these paragraphs are primarily descriptive, how does the tone of each influence our understanding or imply a bias?

VERSION A:

The haunting beauty of the U.S.S. *Arizona* Memorial, which seems to float on the clear blue waters of Pearl Harbor in Hawaii, is a perfect testimony to the tragedy that took place on December 7, 1941. Visitors linger over the names inscribed in the white marble, respectfully whispering. Some search for names, and others search the waters, staring at the rusting remains of the battleship U.S.S. *Arizona*. As the National Park Service Web site reminds us, this national shrine "symbolizes American sacrifice and resolve." As visit to this shrine is a reminder of lives lost, of young men whose futures were canceled but whose sacrifice will not be forgotten.

VERSION B:

The solemn beauty of the U.S.S. *Arizona* Memorial, which hovers on the calmly indifferent blue waters of Pearl Harbor in Hawaii, is a grim testimony to the horrifying tragedy that took place on December 7, 1941. As I wandered through the memorial, I saw visitors glance at the names inscribed in the white marble and cast their eyes downward, avoiding the look of others. Some visitors search for names, and others search the waters, staring at the rusting remains of the battleship U.S.S. *Arizona*. I looked for the name of a friend's father but could not find it. The National Park Service Web site reminds us that this national shrine "symbolizes American sacrifice and resolve," but the faces of a few elderly visitors tell another story. They seem to be remembering a day of infamy that they feel guilty for surviving, while other young men, their comrades-in-arms, never returned to fulfill their lives.

Chapter 2 Reading Texts

Exercise A   2b Highlighting a Text

Using the Checklist: Using Highlighting Symbols in your handbook, highlight the passage below. When you have finished highlighting the text, answer the questions that follow.

The early history of Islam is a turbulent one. Though, ironically, the name *Islam* means "peace," early followers of the prophet and leader Muhammad faced persecution and exile. After his death, the number of believers increased, and the faith spread throughout the Middle East, but controversies over leadership and interpretation of the holy text led to continued warfare and divisiveness.

In AD 610, the prophet Muhammad received the first revelations that would become the Qu'ran (also Koran), the sacred text of his followers, people who would be known as Muslims. Muhammad was living in Mecca, in today's Saudi Arabia, but persecution of his converts led to the migration, or *hijrah*, from Mecca to Medina. Warfare between the Muslims and those who lived in Mecca continued until the Treaty of Hudaybiyyah between Mecca and Medina in 628.

After the death of the prophet Muhammad in 632, leadership passed into the hands of caliphs, and Muslim armies invaded Iraq, Syria, and Egypt. In 638, the Muslims conquered Jerusalem, which became the third holy city after Mecca and Medina. Although the Qu'ran preached peace, disagreements among caliphs resulted in continuous warfare. Early divisions within Islam led to the factions that exist today.

In 680, a group of Muslims in Kufah who called themselves the Shiah i-Ali, or Partisans of Ali, became the group we now know as Shi'ites. Followers of other seventh-century caliphs included the Karajites and Umayyads. For a while, the Umayyads ruled Jerusalem, but another faction, the Abbasids, joined forces with the Shiis. By the mid-eighth century, Baghdad had become the Abbasid capital. Sufi mystics, the "drunken Sufis" and "sober Sufis," began to emerge in the ninth and tenth centuries.

Numerous Islamic dynasties throughout the Middle East and as far west as Spain developed over the next two centuries. The power of the caliphs diminished, and local rulers maintained power. By the end of the eleventh century, Western Christians entered the picture when Byzantine emperor Alexius Comnenus asked for help against the

Seljuk Turks and the First Crusade began. The Crusaders conquered Jerusalem in 1099. A religion of peace experienced five centuries of war, with many more to come.

1. What is the purpose of this passage?

   _____

   _____

   _____

2. What is the subject?

   _____

   _____

   _____

3. What is the main idea?

   _____

   _____

   _____

4. How are connections made between ideas?

   _____

   _____

   _____

Source for facts: Karen Armstrong, *Islam: A Short History*. Rev. ed. New York: Modern Library, 2002.

Chapter 3 | Reading Visuals

Exercise A   3a-b Interpreting and Previewing Visuals

Go to the Web site for *Time* magazine at www.time.com and follow their links to the Photo of the Week. Select one or more photos for analysis. Refer to your handbook, Chapter 3, Checklist: Reading Visuals, and apply those criteria to your analysis of the selected photos.

The following activities, based on the criteria in the Checklist: Reading Visuals, may be used for the photo analysis:

1. Have individual students select photos, project them in the classroom, and present an oral analysis.

2. Form panels of 3 to 4 students to select a photo for analysis. Project the photo in the classroom and present an oral analysis.

3. Use a selected photo for an in-class, impromptu writing assignment.

4. Use a selected photo or pair of photos for an essay assignment.

Chapter 4 — Planning an Essay

Exercise A   4b Computers and the Writing Process

Sometimes the material from an essay may also be turned into a presentation. The following is a set of six Powerpoint slides created from the text of Exercise A: 2a Highlighting a Text from Chapter 2. Converting an essay involves understanding the hierarchy of your ideas, similar to the form of an outline (see *Handbook*, Chapter 5c and d), and enhancing the ideas with visual support. Answer the questions below the slide set and then create a presentation from one of your own writing assignments.

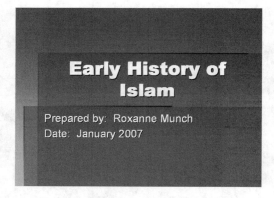

The Prophet Muhammad

- A.D. 610—the Prophet Muhammad received his first revelations.
  - Revelations became the sacred text or Qu'ran.
  - People became known as Muslims.
  - Persecution of followers led to *hijrah* from Mecca to Medina.
- A.D. 628—Treaty of Hudaybiyyah between Mecca and Medina.
- A.D. 632—Muhammad dies.

Conquests under the Caliphs

- Caliphs assume leadership.
- Muslim armies invade Iraq, Syria, and Egypt.
- A.D. 638—Muslims conquer Jerusalem.
- Three cities sacred to Muslims:
  - Mecca
  - Medina
  - Jerusalem
- Early factions lead to continuous warfare.

Early Divisions of Islam

- A.D. 680—Muslims in Kufah become known as Shi'ites.
- Followers of other caliphs become Karajites and Umayyads.
- Baghdad is capital of Abbasids.
- Sufi mystics emerge.

The First Crusade

- Power of caliphs diminishes.
- Local rulers maintain power.
- Byzantine emperor Alexius Comnenus calls for help.
  - Involves Western Europe.
  - Opposes Seljuk Turks.
- 1099—First Crusaders conquer Jerusalem.
- Five centuries of war follow.

1. What does the title of the presentation tell us about what is to follow? Who created the presentation? When?

2. What is the purpose of slide #2? How is it related to the rest of the presentation? Why have a slide of this type?

3. What is the relationship of the slides to the text of the essay? Why were the slides divided in this manner?

4. What is the relationship of the first and second levels of bulleted points?

5. How is parallelism used in this presentation?

6. This presentation has no graphics. What types of graphics might enhance the presentation?

7. Is anything missing in the slide presentation that was important in the essay?

Chapter 4 Planning an Essay

Exercise B   4d Choosing and Narrowing a Topic

The following table provides a course, a purpose, and an assignment. Create a topic suitable for a 500- to 750-word essay.

Course	Purpose	Assignment	Topic
American Literature	Inform	Select one American author of the nineteenth century and write about his or her family and educational background.	
Ethics	Persuade	Take a stand on a current ethical issue.	
Creative Writing	Express	Write about an incident you experienced between the ages of 12 and 14.	
Foreign Language	Inform	Identify a cultural monument for the language you are studying and write about its history.	
Astronomy	Inform	Select one planet and explain its physical traits.	
Computer Science	Evaluate	Select a software program and evaluate its usefulness and accessibility.	
Genetics	Persuade	Select a controversial topic in genetics and argue a position.	

Chapter 5	**Using a Thesis to Shape Your Material**

Exercise A   **5b Developing a Thesis**

Read the following statements and indicate whether they qualify as an effective thesis. Use these notations to indicate areas that need improvement. Discuss ways to revise statements with potential for development.

> A = Announcement
> F = Statement of fact
> G = General subject
> ET = Effective thesis

_____ 1. The Jack Daniel's Distillery is in Tennessee.

_____

_____

_____

_____

_____

_____

_____

_____ 2. A tour of the Jack Daniel's Distillery is an interesting
           learning experience.

_____

_____

_____

_____

_____

_____

_____

_____ 3. This paper will cover the steps in the process of creating Jack Daniel's whiskey.

_____

_____

_____

_____

_____

_____

_____ 4. I visited the Jack Daniel's Distillery on our family vacation.

_____

_____

_____

_____

_____

_____ 5. The tour guides at the Jack Daniel's Distillery provide a snapshot of American history and Yankee ingenuity.

_____

_____

_____

_____

_____

_____ 6. Jack Daniel had what he needed to make whiskey: a water supply, a fuel supply, and a grain supply.

_____

_____

_____

_____

_____

_____ 7. Jack Daniel's uses a square bottle so that it will not roll around.

_____

_____

_____

_____

_____ 8. I will analyze the sanitation procedures used in the production of Jack Daniel's whiskey.

_____

_____

_____

_____

_____

_____ 9. Today, computers are used extensively to monitor whiskey production at Jack Daniel's Distillery.

_____

_____

_____

_____

_____

_____

_____10. Listing the Jack Daniel's Distillery on the Historic Register makes a mockery of American history.

_____

_____

_____

_____

_____

_____

Chapter 5 | Using a Thesis to Shape Your Material

Exercise B   5b Developing a Thesis

Read the following statements and indicate whether they qualify as an effective thesis. Use these notations to indicate the areas needing improvement. Discuss ways to revise statements with potential for development.

A = Announcement
F = Statement of fact
G = General subject
ET = Effective thesis

_____ 1.   One of Michelangelo's most famous works is the Sistine Chapel's ceiling in the Vatican.

_____

_____

_____

_____

_____

_____

_____ 2.   The twentieth-century restoration of the ceiling of the Sistine Chapel is garish and damaging to the authenticity of the work.

_____

_____

_____

_____

_____

_____ 3. Most people recognize the scene where man is created.

_____

_____

_____

_____

_____

_____

_____ 4. The Sistine Chapel's ceiling is one of the greatest works of
        art in the world.

_____

_____

_____

_____

_____

_____ 5. The sibyls pictured on the ceiling are wise women from
        mythology who spoke prophecies.

_____

_____

_____

_____

_____ 6. The most famous sibyl is the Cumaean Sibyl.

_____ 7. Fresco, the technique used by Michelangelo, is painting on wet plaster.

_____ 8. This paper will explain the religious significance of Michelangelo's portrayal of selected prophets on the Sistine Chapel's ceiling.

_____

_____

_____

_____ 9. I think the most moving part of the ceiling is the casting
out of Adam and Eve from Paradise.

_____

_____

_____

_____

_____10. Michelangelo's choice to alternate Old Testament prophets
with sibyls of the ancient world shows sensitivity to the
spiritual roles of both men and women.

_____

_____

_____

_____

_____

_____

Chapter 5	**Using a Thesis to Shape Your Material**

Exercise C	**5d Constructing a Formal Outline**

Using the topics you developed for Chapter 4, Exercise B, construct a formal topic outline. Use three levels of headings, and follow the guidelines in Chapter 5d. Then, using the same information, create a formal sentence outline.

 After constructing your outlines, use the following checklist to review your work and to revise the appropriate parts of the outline.

- ☐ Did you state your thesis?

- ☐ Did you have at least two subheadings in any category?

- ☐ Have you used the appropriate letter or number for the heading level? Did you follow it with a period?

- ☐ Did you capitalize the first word of each entry?

- ☐ Are all headings of the same rank grammatically parallel?

_____

_____

_____

_____

_____

_____

_____

_____

_____

_____

_____

_____

Chapter 5 — Using a Thesis to Shape Your Material

Exercise D — 5d Constructing a Formal Outline Using Presentation Software

Inspired by the *Pirates of the Caribbean* movies, you have researched the topic of pirates and discovered some historical material. You have formed a working thesis that the lives of historical pirates were not as glamorous as the movie portrayals. You also have the following historical information in the form of rough notes. Please do the following:

1. Finalize your thesis.

2. Construct a formal outline with the information below. Choose your own pattern of organization, or try several different ones. You may wish to organize chronologically, by each individual pirate, by comparing reality and fiction, or by categories of information. Omit any irrelevant information.

3. Create an electronic presentation with graphics from the formal outline.

4. Do more research and write an essay on the topic.

NOTES ON PIRATES

- Some terms: Pirates = Caribbean; corsairs = Mediterranean; privateers = authorized or commissioned by governments to attack vessels of enemy nations

- Some dates: 1701—Captain Kidd executed; 1688—Henry Morgan dies; 1718—Blackbeard dies; 1720—Anne Bonny and Mary Read tried

- Some famous pirates: Sir Henry Morgan; Captain Kidd; Mary Read and Anne Bonny; Edward Teach or Blackbeard (also fictional pirates: Captain Hook and Long John Silver)

- Forms of death: Morgan died of natural causes in Jamaica; Kidd hung in chains; Read and Bonny reprieved because pregnant; Blackbeard killed in battle on ship

- Literature and movies: *Peter Pan, Treasure Island, The Black Pirate* (silent film with Douglas Fairbanks; 1926), *The Black Swan* (Tyrone Power, 1942), *The Buccaneer* (1938), *Pirates of the Caribbean* (2 films)

Chapter 6 — Drafting and Revising

Exercise A   6c Using Specific Revision Strategies

The following passage is a draft of a section from a research paper on portrayals of women in comedy. Assume that it is yours and that it has been annotated electronically by your instructor. You need to revise it and prepare for a conference. Revise the passage and then prepare for the conference by using the Comments function to raise your own questions. Apply the Checklist: Getting the Most out of a Conference from your *Handbook*, Chapter 6.

PORTRAYALS OF WOMEN IN COMEDY

While characters of both genders and all ages and social classes are objects of ridicule in a wide range of comedies, women experience limitations much more restrictive than males of their own class. Even the female characters who participate in the celebrations of comedy as fiancées and brides are limited to only one possibility for happiness and fulfillment, and the older females who portray wives and "old maids" are victims of merciless stereotyping and ridicule. As Erich Segal notes, the earliest bit of comic dialogue is anti-wife: "Misogynistic humor entered comedy via the long tradition of iambic poetry" (Segal 29). [In Greek New Comedy, the types were very specifically defined and portrayed through the masks they wore. As Harry Levin explains, the rigidity of the types conveyed by masks and the consequent structuring of the *dramatis personae* limits possibilities and assumes no likelihood of change.

> **Comment [RM1]:** New paragraph here?

The early actor—originally an amateur–derived his personality from his mask, even as our word itself derives from *persona*, the Latin noun for mask, . . . In New Comedy [the masks] represented social types. There were exactly forty-four of these, according to the rhetorician Pollux; and the distribution was an interesting reflection of the *dramatis personae*, if not of society at large: ten old men, ten young men, three old women, fourteen young women, and seven slaves. [(Levin 63)

> **Comment [RM2]:** Edit this quotation. Do you need this part?

> **Deleted:** Each of them was costumed in an appropriate color, depending on age, sex, and status. That is not an extensive but rather a limited number, if we assume that drama should present in some fullness the permutations and the interactions of human behavior. It committed dramatists to the assumption that human nature changed little from one epoch to the next.

Levin surveys the tradition of stereotypes and indicates that, while some playwrights found them confining, most continued to rely on them. The list was often itemized in the prologues of plays by Terence, Plautus, and others: "*senex, adulescens, servus, parasitus, matrona, virgo, ancilla, meretrix, et caetera*" (Levin 63–64). For women characters, virgin, wife, or whore were the options, with ideals of chastity and faithfulness promoted and rewarded on the one hand, and faithlessness and promiscuity ridiculed and punished on the other. Erich Segal claims the problem stereotype, above all, is the "*uxor dotata*, the henpecking, big-dowried *matrona* who makes her husband's life a misery" (Segal 190). Another problem stereotype with similar traits is the mother-in-law figure, whom Segal discusses in his chapter on Terence's *Hecyra (Mother-in-Law)*. "Since the earliest days of the theater, the stage mother-in-law has been a perennial figure of fun, an agelast whose only joy in life is making the happily-ever-afters miserable. The *belle-mere* was a familiar figure on the nineteenth-century French stage, always frantically scheming to be a spoilsport to the young lovers" (Segal 241). Segal also notes, however, that Terence's character, Sostrata, is a sympathetic and caring mother-in-law. The play was also a failure in its own time. Segal praises the play for its handling of suspense, but he also suspects that it was difficult for the Roman audience to have clear expectations, as they were accustomed to, about the mother-in-law character. The implications of Segal's interpretation are that comedy may only succeed when the expectations are founded on traditional representations of characters that do not confuse the audience. This view effectively eliminates the possibility of change.

> **Comment [RM3]:** We don't have a context for this clause. Is it needed?

> **Comment [RM4]:** You're spending time on a play that very few people would know. Either explain it more fully or delete the discussion.

> **Comment [RM5]:** This statement is quite a generalization. Think further about the implications of Segal's interpretation.

Another stereotype from Roman comedy promotes both feminine chastity and loyalty, which denies or degrades a woman's own sexual and personal desires as inappropriate and even immoral. Romans valued female chastity, even into widowhood: "The Romans surpassed the Greeks in their reverence for female chastity, and a Roman matron was praised for being *univira* (the actual term is of a later era). This meant that the 'chaste' widows were not supposed to remarry" (Segal 218). The sentimental, tearful comedy is also a prototype of the suffering woman, the "patient Griselda" type. Segal discusses the Terentian phrase *hinc illae lacrimae* and states, "The literal 'hence these tears' only approximates the delicacy which could serve as a motto for Terentian dramaturgy" (Segal 233).

> **Comment [RM6]:** You're relying very heavily on Segal and not adding enough of your own analysis in this paragraph.

Overall, gender bias at the expense of women is a mainstay of Roman comedy: "The animus against women is so pervasive in Roman comedy that even slaves take any opportunity to rail at the opposite sex" (Segal 190). Even as late as 1962, in his musical *A Funny Thing Happened on the Way to the Forum*, Stephen Sondheim mockingly uses the same formula he found in three Plautine comedies for stereotyped female characters named to match their traits: Domina the overbearing matron, Philia the young virgin, and an entire house of prostitution owned by Lycus and occupied by women named for their specific talents—Tintinabula, Panacea, the Geminae, Vibrata, and Gymnasia. In the first act, the prostitutes, dressed to enhance their particular "gifts," are paraded for Hero, the young hero. Even as the mid-twentieth-century movements toward civil rights and gender equity were developing, Sondheim's musical, with its classic stereotypes, was an award-winning Broadway success. The familiar stereotypes bring laughter and entertainment, partly for the metacomic exaggeration that the more sophisticated audience members would recognize, but once again at the expense of women.

> **Comment [RM7]:** Explain more fully.

Chapter 7	Writing Paragraphs

Exercise A	7a Writing Unified Paragraphs

Read the following paragraphs and then for each,

1. Label the topic sentence TS.
2. Delete the sentence that does not fit the paragraph.

PARAGRAPH A

The game of chess has two traditions: a form played with abstract pieces and another form played with elaborate pieces. The abstract pieces are common to the Islamic world, where chess was played as a war game long before it arrived in Western Europe. Pieces of carved ivory, bone, stone, crystal, or even ceramic were used. In contrast, or-nately carved figures representing human forms appeared in Europe during the Middle Ages. An elaborately carved set of ivory chessmen is associated with Charlemagne, and the set is believed to have been made in a workshop during the eleventh century in Italy. By the twelfth century, two-colored boards came into use.

PARAGRAPH B

A set of eighty-two pieces known as the Lewis Chessman was found in a hoard in Uig on the west coast of the Isle of Lewis in the Outer Hebrides, a set of islands northwest of Scotland, some time in 1831. Evidence on the surfaces of the pieces suggests that they were located in a sand dune. The surfaces also suggest that tiny sand ter-mites burrowed in the dune. The pieces do not show evidence of damage from seawater, but several have cracks and other flaws, prob-ably caused by changes in climate and dampness.

PARAGRAPH C

The Lewis chessmen are detailed anthropomorphic walrus tusk figures, fully carved on all sides. The kings are seated on thrones and hold sheathed swords across their laps. Their thrones are decorated with foliage and carvings of beasts. The queens are similarly seated on elaborate thrones, but each queen rests her head on her right hand. Some bishops are seated and others stand. They wear vest-ments and miters, hold croziers, and in some cases hold books. The knights ride horses, carry shields in their left hands, and hold spears in their right hands. They wear full armor. The pawns are plain shapes that do not have human forms. The last human figures are standing warders bearing shields and raised swords.

Source for information for all exercises in Chapter 7: Neil Stratford, *The Lewis Chessmen and the Enigma of the Hoard*. London: British Museum Press, 1997.

Chapter 7	**Writing Paragraphs**

Exercise B	**7b Writing Coherent Paragraphs**

Read the following paragraph, which is adapted from the preceding exercise, and then answer the questions below it. Sentences are numbered for easy identification.

(1) The Lewis chessmen are detailed anthropomorphic walrus tusk figures, human shapes fully carved on all sides. (2) The kings are seated on thrones and hold sheathed swords across their laps. (3) **Their** thrones are decorated with foliage and carvings of beasts. (4) The queens are similarly seated on elaborate thrones, but each queen rests her head on her right hand. (5) Some bishops are seated and others stand. (6) **They** wear vestments and miters, hold croziers, and in some cases hold books. (7) The knights ride horses, carry shields in their left hands, and hold spears in their right hands. (8) **They** wear full armor. (9) The last human figures are standing warders bearing shields and raised swords.

1. Identify the parallelism within sentences 2, 3, 4, 5, 6, and 7.

   _____

   _____

   _____

2. Identify the parallelism between sentences 2, 4, 5, and 7.

   _____

   _____

   _____

3. What is the device indicated in bold in sentences 3, 6, and 8? How does it support coherence?

   _____

_____

_____

_____

4. How is repetition used in sentence 1? What is clarified?

_____

_____

_____

Chapter 7 | Writing Paragraphs

Exercise C | 7c Writing Well-Developed Paragraphs

Read the following paragraph and then chart the paragraph structure, as shown in your handbook, Chapter 7c.

The game of chess has two traditions: a form played with abstract pieces and another form played with elaborate pieces. The abstract pieces are common to the Islamic world, where chess was played as a war game long before it arrived in Western Europe. Pieces of carved ivory, bone, stone, crystal, or even ceramic were used. In contrast, ornately carved figures representing human forms appeared in Europe during the Middle Ages. One elaborately carved set of ivory chessmen is associated with Charlemagne, and the set is believed to have been made in a workshop during the eleventh century in Italy. Less ornate but clearly human figures appear throughout Western Europe in the late Middle Ages.

_____

_____

_____

_____

_____

_____

_____

_____

_____

| Chapter 7 | **Writing Paragraphs** |

Exercise D   **7d Patterns of Paragraph Development**

Read the following paragraphs and identify the major pattern of development for each. The first three paragraphs are modified from the preceding exercises.

PARAGRAPH A

The game of chess has two traditions: a form played with abstract pieces and another form played with elaborate pieces. The abstract pieces are common to the Islamic world, where chess was played as a war game long before it arrived in Western Europe. Pieces of carved ivory, bone, stone, crystal, or even ceramic were used. In contrast, ornately carved figures representing human forms appeared in Europe during the Middle Ages. An elaborately carved set of ivory chessmen is associated with Charlemagne, and the set is believed to have been made in a workshop during the eleventh century in Italy. While the styles of the chess pieces vary, the game is always a representation of battle.

Pattern: _____

_____

_____

_____

_____

_____

_____

_____

_____

PARAGRAPH B

A set of eighty-two pieces known as the Lewis chessmen was found in a hoard in Uig, on the west coast of the Isle of Lewis in the Outer Hebrides some time in 1831. While the origins of the pieces are unknown, study of them provides some insight into their survival. Evidence on the surfaces of the pieces suggests that they were located in a sand dune. The surfaces also suggest that tiny sand termites burrowed in the dune. The pieces do not show evidence of damage from seawater, but several have cracks and other flaws, probably caused by changes in climate and dampness.

Pattern: _____

_____

_____

_____

_____

_____

_____

_____

_____

PARAGRAPH C

The Lewis chessmen are detailed anthropomorphic walrus tusk figures, fully carved on all sides. The kings are seated on thrones and hold sheathed swords across their laps. Their thrones are decorated with foliage and carvings of beasts. The queens are similarly seated on elaborate thrones, but each queen rests her head on her right hand. Some bishops are seated and others stand. They wear vestments and miters, hold croziers, and, in some cases, hold books. The knights ride horses, carry shields in their left hands, and hold spears in their right hands. They wear full armor. The pawns are plain shapes that do not have human forms. The last human figures are standing warders bearing shields and raised swords.

Pattern: _____

_____

_____

_____

_____

_____

_____

_____

_____

_____

PARAGRAPH D

The sixteen surviving bishops of the Lewis chessmen include seven seated figures and nine standing ones. They all wear mitres, the traditional pointed bishop's headdress with two ribbons hanging from the back. Their garments include either the tunicle and cope or the complete clerical vestments of tunicle, cope, stole, and chasuble. They carry the crozier or crooked bishop's staff. The seated bishops' thrones are elaborately carved with latticework, scrolls, or interlacing foliage on the sides and back. The figures vary because the walrus tusks from which they were carved also varied in size and coloration.

Pattern: _____

_____

_____

_____

_____

_____

Chapter 7   Writing Paragraphs

The following short essay was used for annotating in Exercise A of Chapter 2. Reread the essay and determine its purpose: to inform, reflect, evaluate, or persuade. Then, identify the various patterns used to develop the paragraphs and the essay overall.

1 The early history of Islam is a turbulent one. Though, ironically, the name *Islam* means "peace," early followers of the prophet and leader Muhammad faced persecution and exile. After his death, the number of believers increased, and the faith spread throughout the Middle East, but controversies over leadership and interpretation of the holy text led to continued warfare and divisiveness.

2 In AD 610, the prophet Muhammad received the first revelations that would become the Qu'ran (also Koran), the sacred text of his followers, people who would be known as Muslims. Muhammad was living in Mecca, in today's Saudi Arabia, but persecution of his converts led to their migration, or *hijrah*, from Mecca to Medina. Warfare between the Muslims and those who lived in Mecca continued until the Treaty of Hudaybiyyah between Mecca and Medina in 628.

3 After the death of the prophet Muhammad in 632, leadership passed into the hands of caliphs, and Muslim armies invaded Iraq, Syria, and Egypt. In 638, the Muslims conquered Jerusalem, which became the third holy city after Mecca and Medina. Although the Qu'ran preached peace, disagreements among caliphs resulted in continuous warfare. Early divisions within Islam led to the factions that exist today.

4 In 680, a group of Muslims in Kufah called themselves the Shiah i-Ali, or Partisans of Ali, became the group we know as Shi'ites. Followers of other seventh-century caliphs included the Karajites and Umayyads. For a while, the Umayyads ruled Jerusalem, but another faction, the Abbasids, joined forces with the Shiis. By the mid-eighth century, Baghdad had become the Abbasid capital. Sufi mystics, the "drunken Sufis" and "sober Sufis," began to emerge in the ninth and tenth centuries.

5 Numerous Islamic dynasties throughout the Middle East and as far west as Spain developed over the next two centuries. The power of the caliphs diminished, and local rulers maintained power. By the end of the eleventh century, Western Christians entered the picture when Byzantine emperor Alexius Comnenus asked for help against the Seljuk Turks and the First Crusade began. The Crusaders conquered Jerusalem in 1099. A religion of peace experienced five centuries of war, with many more to come.

Essay's purpose: _____

_____

_____

_____

_____

_____

Pattern(s) in ¶1: _____

_____

_____

_____

_____

_____

Pattern(s) in ¶2: _____

_____

_____

_____

_____

_____

Pattern(s) in ¶3: _____

_____

_____

_____

_____

_____

Pattern(s) in ¶4: _____

_____

_____

_____

_____

Pattern(s) in ¶5: _____

_____

_____

_____

_____

_____

Patterns in entire essay: _____

_____

_____

_____

_____

_____

_____

_____

_____

_____

_____

_____

Chapter 8 | Thinking Critically

Exercise A | 8a Distinguishing Fact from Opinion

Identify each statement with an *F* for *Fact* or an *O* for *Opinion*.

_____ 1. Gwendolyn Brooks, African-American poet, was born in Topeka, Kansas, and grew up in Chicago.

_____ 2. Alice Walker stated, "If there was ever a born poet, I think it is Brooks."

_____ 3. If there was ever a born poet, I think it is Brooks.

_____ 4. Brooks writes of the black experience.

_____ 5. Brooks writes of the black woman's experience of abortion in haunting, painful language in "the mother."

_____ 6. Brooks's poem entitled "the mother" uses a speaker who has experienced an abortion.

_____ 7. "We Real Cool" is probably Gwendolyn Brooks's most famous poem.

_____ 8. "We Real Cool" was printed on some of the CTA buses in Chicago.

_____ 9. Brooks was the first African American to receive the Pulitzer Prize for poetry.

_____10. Brooks creates a fictional setting she calls Bronzeville for many of her poems.

Chapter 8 — Thinking Critically

Exercise B   8c Detecting Bias

Using the Checklist: Detecting Bias in your handbook, identify the biases in the following argument.

Mandatory placement in developmental or remedial courses in math and English should not be allowed in college. After all, college students are adults and should be able to make their own choices. In addition, they are the customers, and the customer is always right. Why should placement tests, which are notoriously biased, be the basis for deciding which courses a student may take.

If a student is forced to take developmental courses, that student may become discouraged and not want to continue with his or her education. It will take so long to get to those college-level courses that the student will just give up. If a student feels ready to tackle courses in history or sociology or biology, why should that student be required to take special reading, writing, and math courses?

Schools try to sugarcoat those courses by calling them "developmental," when they are really meant to treat the student like a dummy and insult his or her intelligence. Students pay good, hard-earned cash for courses, and they should have the right to take whichever courses they wish. College students are adults; they can fight for their country by serving in the military and can vote, so why should they be held back in college? Only they know best what is needed for their success in college.

_____

_____

_____

_____

_____

_____

Chapter 9 | Using Logic

Exercise A | 9a Understanding Inductive Reasoning

Using the following facts, answer the questions below.

FACTS

- 375 students entered Millard Fillmore University as junior-level transfer students from state community colleges during the fall of 2001.
  - 200 are women and 175 are men.
  - This group's average incoming GPA is 2.76.
  - This group's average age is 23.5.
  - 320 graduated in spring 2003 with an average GPA of 2.90.
  - 40 students transferred elsewhere.
  - 15 students apparently dropped out and did not go to any other college or university.

- 340 students entered Millard Fillmore University at the same time as junior-level transfer students from various four-year colleges and universities.
  - 150 are women and 190 are men.
  - This group's average incoming GPA is 2.90.
  - This group's average age is 21.2.
  - 300 graduated in spring 2003 with an average GPA of 2.90.
  - 35 students transferred elsewhere.
  - 5 students apparently dropped out and did not go to any other college or university.

- 600 juniors at Millard Fillmore University during the fall of 2001 have attended only that college since their freshman year.
  - 170 are women and 170 are men.
  - This group's average GPA as they began the junior year is 2.60.
  - This group's average age is 20.8.
  - 400 graduated in spring 2003 with an average GPA of 2.80.
  - 100 students transferred elsewhere.
  - 100 students apparently dropped out and did not go to any other college or university.

QUESTIONS AND INFERENCES

1. Does gender make a difference in graduation rates? Does age make a difference in graduation rates? Can an inference be made? Why or why not?

_____

_____

_____

_____

_____

_____

_____

_____

_____

_____

2. Is there a relationship between GPA at the beginning of the junior year and GPA at graduation? What might account for the differences?

_____

_____

_____

_____

_____

_____

_____

_____

_____

_____

3. Is there a difference between students transferring from other institutions and those who started college at Fillmore—"native" students? Can anything be predicted about transfer students versus native students?

_____

_____

_____

_____

_____

_____

_____

_____

_____

4. Can anything be inferred about dropout rates and schools of origin?

_____

_____

_____

_____

_____

_____

_____

_____

5. Can anything be inferred about the differences between students who transfer from community colleges and those who transfer from other institutions?

_____

_____

_____

_____

_____

_____

_____

_____

_____

Chapter 9	**Using Logic**

Exercise B	**9b Understanding Deductive Reasoning**

Examine each of the following five syllogisms and label them as

    A = True and valid

    B = True but not valid

    C = False but valid

    D = False and not valid

_____ 1. Elevated cholesterol definitely causes heart attacks and strokes.
Jordan had a heart attack.
Jordan must have elevated cholesterol.

_____ 2. All the American presidents of the twentieth century were elected to office.
Gerald Ford was president in the twentieth century.
Gerald Ford was elected to office.

_____ 3. Shakespearean sonnets end in a rhymed couplet.
"'Twas the Night Before Christmas" ends in a rhymed couplet.
"'Twas the Night Before Christmas" is a Shakespearean sonnet.

_____ 4. Shakespearean sonnets end in a rhymed couplet.
"[My Mistress' Eyes are Nothing Like the Sun]" is a Shakespearean sonnet.
"[My Mistress' Eyes are Nothing Like the Sun]" ends in a rhymed couplet.

_____ 5. Ravens can be trained to talk.
Michael was trained to talk.
Michael is a raven.

Chapter 9	**Using Logic**

Exercise C   9d Recognizing Logical Fallacies

Identify the logical fallacy in each of the following statements.

The fallacies listed below are identified and defined in Chapter 9d of your handbook. Practice your knowledge of logical fallacies by identifying the fallacy in each of the statements below; then, give a short reason for your choice.

- Hasty generalization
- Sweeping generalization/stereotype
- Equivocation
- *Non sequitur* (does not follow)
- Either/or fallacy
- *Post hoc, ergo propter hoc* (after this, therefore because of this)
- Begging the question or circular reasoning
- False analogy
- Red herring
- Argument to ignorance *(argumentum ad ignorantiam)*
- Bandwagon fallacy
- Argument to the person *(ad hominem)*
- Argument to the people *(ad populum)*

1. Alex says he has had more luck getting dates with girls since he stopped working at the computer center. He says that girls obviously thought he was a nerd because he worked there.

   _____

   _____

   _____

   _____

   _____

   _____

   _____

2. If you really loved me, you'd spend our anniversary here at home instead of going on that business trip.

_____

_____

_____

_____

_____

_____

3. Making condoms available in high schools is like giving a thief a license to steal.

_____

_____

_____

_____

_____

_____

4. Her repeated failure to find a job clearly indicates that she lacks ambition.

_____

_____

_____

_____

_____

_____

5. I'd be getting all "A's" in my classes if my parents would buy me a laptop computer.

_____

_____

_____

_____

_____

_____

6. Since he avoided being drafted during the Vietnam War, Joe Blow has no right to be Commander-in-Chief of the Armed Forces. Therefore, we should not vote for him for President.

_____

_____

_____

_____

_____

_____

7. My parents taught us that if we did our very best on every job, we would never be without a job.

_____

_____

_____

_____

_____

_____

_____

8. Either you are for us or you are against us in this time of national crisis.

_____

_____

_____

_____

_____

_____

9. His ugly attitude is unmatched by anything except his ugly face.

_____

_____

_____

_____

_____

10. Shopping at Old Navy will definitely make you more popular.

_____

_____

_____

Chapter 10	**Writing Argumentative Essays**

Exercise A	**10a Planning an Argumentative Essay**

Using the topics listed below, prepare two argumentative thesis statements, one defending the issue and one refuting or disagreeing with the first position.

1. Using ACT or SAT scores as the basis for college admission

   Thesis 1 _____

   _____

   Thesis 2 _____

   _____

2. Shopping at stores that import goods from countries that use child labor

   Thesis 1 _____

   _____

   Thesis 2 _____

   _____

3. Being vegetarian

   Thesis 1 _____

   _____

   Thesis 2 _____

   _____

4. Using laboratory animals for testing cosmetics

   Thesis 1 _____

   _____

Thesis 2 _____

_____

5. Keeping an exotic pet

   Thesis 1 _____

   _____

   Thesis 2 _____

   _____

6. Body piercing and/or tattooing for people over 18

   Thesis 1 _____

   _____

   Thesis 2 _____

   _____

7. Giving tax breaks for parents sending children to private or
   parochial schools

   Thesis 1 _____

   _____

   Thesis 2 _____

   _____

8. Instituting prayer in public schools

   Thesis 1 _____

   _____

   Thesis 2 _____

   _____

9. Changing the age for completion of high school with a diploma to 16

Thesis 1 _____

_____

Thesis 2 _____

_____

10. Using public school gyms to house the homeless at night

Thesis 1 _____

_____

Thesis 2 _____

_____

11. Changing our national anthem from "The Star-Spangled Banner" to "America the Beautiful"

Thesis 1 _____

_____

Thesis 2 _____

_____

Chapter 10 | Writing Argumentative Essays

Exercise B   10b Using Evidence Effectively

Using the topics listed below and the argumentative thesis statements you created in Exercise A, provide three to five reasons to support the position. Then, supply reasons to refute the opposing views.

1. Using ACT or SAT scores as the basis for college admission

PRO	CON
1.	1.
2.	2.
3.	3.
4.	4.
5.	5.

2. Shopping at stores that import goods from countries that use child labor

PRO	CON
1.	1.
2.	2.
3.	3.
4.	4.
5.	5.

3. Being vegetarian

PRO	CON
1.	1.
2.	2.
3.	3.
4.	4.
5.	5.

4. Using laboratory animals for testing cosmetics

PRO	CON
1.	1.
2.	2.
3.	3.
4.	4.
5.	5.

5. Keeping an exotic pet

PRO	CON
1.	1.
2.	2.
3.	3.
4.	4.
5.	5.

6. Body piercing and/or tattooing for people over 18

PRO	CON
1.	1.
2.	2.
3.	3.
4.	4.
5.	5.

7. Giving tax breaks for parents sending children to private or parochial schools

PRO	CON
1.	1.
2.	2.
3.	3.
4.	4.
5.	5.

8. Instituting prayer in public schools

PRO	CON
1.	1.
2.	2.
3.	3.
4.	4.
5.	5.

9. Changing the age for completion of high school with a diploma to 16

PRO	CON
1.	1.
2.	2.
3.	3.
4.	4.
5.	5.

10. Using public school gyms to house the homeless at night

PRO	CON
1.	1.
2.	2.
3.	3.
4.	4.
5.	5.

11. Changing our national anthem from "The Star-Spangled Banner" to "America the Beautiful"

PRO	CON
1.	1.
2.	2.
3.	3.
4.	4.
5.	5.

Chapter 11 | Using Visuals to Support Your Arguments

Exercise A | 11b Evaluating Visuals

The following four graphics all represent the same information, also available in Exercise A: 9e for Chapter 9. The color-coding of series varies in the bar graphs.

1. Using the information in the table below, determine which groups are represented in which series in each bar graph.

2. Which graph would be the most effective or least effective for recruiting students to Millard Fillmore University (MFU)? Why?

3. Which students have the best chance of graduating with a degree?

Graduation, Transfers, and Withdrawals at Millard Fillmore University

Starting Point	Graduates	Transfers	Withdrawals
Junior-year transfers from 2-year colleges	320	40	15
Junior-year transfers from universities	300	35	5
Juniors with 2 years at MFU (native students)	400	100	100
TOTALS	1020	175	120

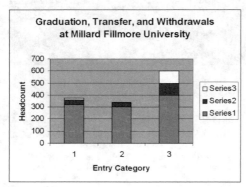

Figure 1

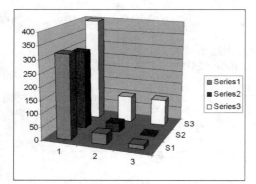

Figure 2

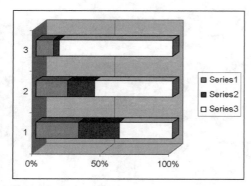

Figure 3

Chapter 12 Writing Electronic Arguments

Exercise A   12a Considering Audience and Purpose

Search www.amazon.com for a book you have read recently. Go to the reviews and do the following:

1. Read the reviews already posted. Respond to at least one.

2. Examine the postings and discuss in small groups. Try to discern each reviewer's intended audience and purpose. Consider the following:
   a. Is the review favorable or unfavorable? Do you feel encouraged to read this book?
   b. Is the level of diction complex or simple? Is the intended audience more academic or more oriented toward reading for entertainment?
   c. Is the review written in a personal voice or a formal voice? How can you tell? How would a reader respond to the voice?

3. Write your own review of the book you have selected, either individually or with a small group of others. Post your review.

4. Check periodically for responses to your reviews.

Chapter 13	Writing a Research Paper

Exercise A	The Research Paper Log

Either use the tables below or design your own electronic document to maintain a research paper log. The first table is for recording conferences with your instructor or a tutor. You may also want to include time spent collaborating with fellow students. The second table incorporates information from Chapter 11 of your handbook, but it also has a column for time spent on the task and additional tips for time management. Note that certain steps, such as taking notes and drafting, take much more time than other steps, such as assembling a working bibliography.

Table 1 Log of Conferences

Date and Time	Names of Instructor, Tutor, or Peer	Topic Discussed	Results or Outcome

Table 2 Research Paper Log

Activity	Due Date	Daily Log of Time and Activities Completed	Total Time Spent on Task
Moving from a General Assignment to a Narrow Topic (11a) • Did you review the instructor's guidelines? • Do you understand the purpose of the paper? • Did you complete any preliminary readings or other assignments?			

(continued)

Table 2 (Continued)

Activity	Due Date	Daily Log of Time and Activities Completed	Total Time Spent on Task
Mapping Out a Search Strategy (11b)			
• Are any specific sources required or restricted?			
• How much searching can be done on the computer at home?			
• How much searching requires travel or spending time elsewhere?			
• How much time will be needed for searching away from home?			
Doing Exploratory Research and Formulating a Research Question (11c)			
Assembling a Working Bibliography (11d)			
• Did you record all the essential information to prevent backtracking?			
• Did you record a brief evaluation for determining future usefulness?			
Developing a Tentative Thesis (11e)			
• Is your thesis debatable? (10a)			
• Does it meet the requirements of a good thesis? (4b)			

(continued)

Table 2 (Continued)

Activity	Due Date	Daily Log of Time and Activities Completed	Total Time Spent on Task
• Did your initial research suggest that source materials will be available?			
Doing Focused Research (11f)			
• Have you made your sources readily accessible through printing, emailing, and photocopying?			
• Did your assignment specify types and scope of sources?			
• Have you located the required types of sources?			
Taking Notes (11g)			
• Did you apply the checklist in 11g?			
• Will each note make sense a week from now?			
• Will each note make sense in isolation from other notes?			
• How long does it take you to read and take notes on one source?			
• Can you predict your time needs?			
Fine-Tuning the Thesis (11h)			
• Is your thesis still supportable in light of your research?			

(continued)

Table 2 (Continued)

Activity	Due Date	Daily Log of Time and Activities Completed	Total Time Spent on Task
Constructing an Outline (11i)			
• Did you apply the checklist in 11i?			
• Have you stayed focused on your thesis?			
Writing a Rough Draft (11j)			
• How much can you draft at one sitting?			
• How long does it take you to draft one page?			
• Can you predict time needed to complete the draft?			
Revising Your Drafts (11k)			
• Did you apply the checklist in 11k?			
Preparing a Final Draft (11l)			
• Are all your resources in place: a functioning computer and printer, toner, paper, a disk?			
• Are you using a word-processing program that is compatible with other computers?			
• If your computer fails in some way, do you have a backup plan for completion?			

Chapter 13 | Writing a Research Paper

Exercise B | 13f Taking Notes

Examine the following electronic notecards. Answer the questions that follow. Cards are identified for referencing the questions.

Card #1

> **Hawthorne, Nathaniel.** *The Scarlet Letter.* **Ed. Ross C. Murfin. Boston: Bedford Books/St. Martin's P, 1991. 21–201.**
>
> **First view of Hester and scarlet letter**
> "When the young woman—the mother of this child—stood fully revealed before the crowd, it seemed to be her first impulse to clasp the infant closely to her bosom; not so much by an impulse of motherly affection, as that she might thereby conceal a certain token, which was wrought or fastened into her dress. . . . in fine red cloth, surrounded with an elaborate embroidery and fantastic flourishes of gold thread, appeared the letter A" (Hawthorne 57).
>
> [Contrast of letter to the dull surroundings]

Card #2

> **Hawthorne, Nathaniel.** *The Scarlet Letter.* **Ed. Ross C. Murfin. Boston: Bedford Books/St. Martin's P, 1991. 21–201.**
>
> **Description of Pearl**
> Pearl is portrayed as having the "wild-flower prettiness of a peasant-baby" (Hawthorne 82), full of change and energy, with a "trait of passion" (82). In Chapter 6 entitled "Pearl," all the imagery surrounding Pearl suggests she is ephemeral and magical: "airy sprite" (83), "hovering in the air" (83), "like a glimmering light" (83).

Card #3

Blake, Kathleen. "Pure Tess: Hardy on Knowing a Woman." *Studies in English Literature* 22(1982): 689–705.

Hardy's stereotyping of Tess
Blake is concerned that Hardy himself is as guilty as Angel in generalizing and stereotyping women, in particular Tess. Blake states, "Hardy generalizes about Tess and women almost as incautiously as Angel does. After all, he is the one who calls Tess a field-woman pure and simple and maintains that such a woman loses her margin to form part of the landscape while a field-man remains a personality afield. And he is the one who calls such a woman charming" (Blake 699).

[Is Blake confusing Hardy with Angel? Look harder at the narrative voice.]

Card #4

Flynn, Carol Houlihan. "Consumptive Fictions: Cannibalism and Defoe." Rpt. In *Robinson Crusoe* by Daniel Defoe. 2nd ed. Ed. Michael Shinagel. New York: Norton, 1994. 423–32.

Crusoe's growing savagery
"To protect himself from savagery, Crusoe must repeat acts of mastery, colonizing more and more subjects to feed his growing needs" (Flynn 430).
[Flynn traces the many creatures Robinson Crusoe kills on the island and analyzes how each act is savage even while Crusoe thinks he's helping to civilize Friday.]

Card #5

Backscheider, Paula R. "The Crime Wave and *Moll Flanders*." Rpt. In *Moll Flanders* by Daniel Defoe. Ed. Albert J. Rivero. New York: Norton, 2004. 460–71.

Defoe's purpose of usefulness
"Late in his life, Defoe explained that he wrote to be useful. His writing was, he said, 'a Testimony of my good Will to my Fellow Creatures' " (qtd. in Backscheider 460).

1. Examine each citation. Which works are articles? Which works are books? Explain each part of the citation. _____

   _____

2. Why is the quotation on Card #1 indented? _____

   _____

3. What is the purpose of the ellipses in Card #1? _____

   _____

4. What is the purpose of the captions in bold? _____

   _____

5. What is the purpose of the square brackets? _____

   _____

6. In Cards #2 and #3, why is some of the material not in quotation marks?_____

   _____

7. Why does the passage on Card #5 include double and single quotation marks? _____

   _____

Chapter 14 | Using and Evaluating Library Resources

Exercise A   14a–c Library Research

Most college libraries offer a tour of the physical facility and an orientation to the resources. The following questions can be used or adapted for most college libraries.

1. What types of print and other physical resources are available in your library? Acquire a copy of the library's floor plan and learn the locations of reference books, other books, periodicals in print, video and audio recordings, newspapers, microfilm and microfiche films, and rare or noncirculating materials.

_____

_____

_____

_____

_____

_____

_____

_____

_____

2. How do you check out materials in your library? What type of identification do you need? Where is the Circulation Desk? What can you do if a book you need is checked out?

_____

_____

_____

_____

_____

_____

_____

_____

_____

3. What is a database? How is using a database different from researching for Internet materials?

_____

_____

_____

_____

_____

_____

_____

_____

_____

4. What is the name of the database your library uses for locating books? What materials are available through your library's book database? How do you find works beyond the holdings at your college? How do you initiate an interlibrary loan?

_____

_____

_____

_____

_____

_____

_____

_____

_____

_____

5. What databases does your library subscribe to for periodical materials? What materials are available through each database? What can you do to get an article if it appears as "full text"? What if you need an article and only the citation is available? What is an abstract?

_____

_____

_____

_____

_____

_____

_____

_____

6. What cataloging system is used for books at your college? What other system might be used? Who assigns call numbers to a book? How is it done? Will a call number in the same system be identical from library to library?

_____

_____

_____

_____

_____

_____

_____

_____

_____

_____

7. Check the items that are available for circulation at your school library. What are the time limits on circulating materials?

☐ Books _____

☐ Reference books _____

☐ Maps and atlases _____

☐ Periodicals/magazines _____

☐ Reserve materials _____

☐ Videotapes _____

☐ CDs or other recordings _____

☐ Newspapers _____

8. Check the services that are available at your library. Are costs involved?

☐ Photocopying

☐ Printing from a library computer

☐ Emailing from a library computer

☐ Interlibrary loan for books

☐ Interlibrary loan for printed periodicals

☐ Interlibrary loan for videotapes or other media

☐ Copying audiotapes

☐ Copying videotapes

- ☐ Creating CDs
- ☐ Televisions, VCRs, DVD players, CD players, or other equipment for listening and viewing

Chapter 15 | Using and Evaluating Internet Sources

Exercise A   15b Using the World Wide Web for Research

To understand the diverse possibilities for searching the Web, try the following:

1. Make a brief list of specific topics that interest you. Try to include diverse disciplines and time periods, such as topics from literature, natural sciences, social sciences, current events, and ancient history, and a few personal interests or hobbies.

_____

_____

_____

_____

_____

_____

_____

_____

2. Search the same topic on several of the popular search engines listed in section 15b of your handbook. Compare the results, especially of the first items listed in each search. Was there much duplication? Did some sources appear only on one search engine? How many "hits" did each search engine provide for a particular topic?

_____

_____

_____

_____

_____

_____

_____

_____

_____

_____

3. Try using one of the metasearch engines listed in 15b for the same topics.

4. Try using one or two of the specialized search engines also listed in 15b.

5. Was a particular search engine faster or slower than the others?

_____

_____

_____

_____

_____

_____

_____

_____

_____

6. Try narrowing your search. Put quotation marks around a phrase and search again. Use combining keywords, AND, OR, or NOT, to conduct a Boolean search. Try plus or minus signs

with word combinations. How were the results different from your earlier searches?

_____

_____

_____

_____

_____

_____

_____

_____

_____

Chapter 15 | Using and Evaluating Internet Sources

Exercise B   15d Determining Evaluating Internet Sites

Using a popular search engine visit the Web sites for the following. Note the URL for each site and try to determine the site's general purpose.

1. The White House

   URL: _____

   Purpose: _____

   _____

2. The University of Illinois at Champaign–Urbana

   URL: _____

   Purpose: _____

   _____

3. The Sierra Club

   URL: _____

   Purpose: _____

   _____

4. L.L. Bean

   URL: _____

   Purpose: _____

   _____

5. The *New York Times*

   URL: _____

   Purpose: _____

   _____

6. Disney World

   URL: _____

   Purpose: _____

   _____

7. Yellowstone National Park

   URL: _____

   Purpose: _____

   _____

8. Juilliard School

   URL: _____

   Purpose: _____

   _____

9. United States Coast Guard

   URL: _____

   Purpose: _____

   _____

10. American Broadcasting Company (ABC)

    URL: _____

    Purpose: _____

    _____

11. The Modern Language Association (MLA)

    URL: _____

    Purpose: _____

    _____

12. Barnes and Noble

URL: _____

Purpose: _____

_____

13. Los Angeles Police Department

URL: _____

Purpose: _____

_____

14. Mammoth Cave

URL: _____

Purpose: _____

_____

15. Sears

URL: _____

Purpose: _____

_____

Chapter 15 | Using and Evaluating Internet Sites

Exercise C | **15d Evaluating Internet Sites**

Refer to your answers for Chapter 15: Exercise A, and answer the following questions.

1. Why are both Yellowstone and Mammoth Cave part of "nps"? What does "nps" stand for?

   _____

   _____

   _____

   _____

   _____

   _____

2. What is the difference between www.lapd.org and www.lapdonline.org? What is the relationship between these two addresses?

   _____

   _____

   _____

   _____

   _____

3. What happens when you search for the Modern Language Association? Why does the Purdue OWL usually come up first? What is the Purdue OWL? What determines the first item listed on a Web search?

   _____

   _____

_____

_____

_____

_____

_____

_____

_____

_____

Name _____ Date _____ Score _____

Chapter 15 — Using and Evaluating Internet Sources

Exercise D   Evaluating Internet Sites

Go to several or all fifteen Web sites listed in Exercise A or select different sites. If you select sites, try for a variety of URLs. Using the criteria of accuracy, credibility, objectivity, coverage, and stability, answer the questions below, which are specific to the sites.

ACCURACY

1. Are links available to other references? Specify one or two links and try to use them. Did they result in an available link?

_____

_____

_____

_____

_____

_____

2. Is an author or Webmaster identified? What type of contact information is available?

_____

_____

_____

_____

_____

_____

_____

CREDIBILITY

1. Is the site refereed? Does the author or Webmaster provide credentials?

_____

_____

_____

_____

_____

_____

_____

2. Does the sponsoring organization exist apart from its Web presence? Can you identify any organizations that exist on the Web alone?

_____

_____

_____

_____

_____

_____

_____

3. How long has the site existed? When was it last updated?

_____

_____

_____

_____

_____

_____

_____

_____

OBJECTIVITY

1. Is this site trying to sell a product or service? Identify components of the site that may be marketing something to the viewer.

_____

_____

_____

_____

_____

_____

_____

2. Does additional advertising appear on the site?

_____

_____

_____

_____

_____

_____

_____

_____

3. Can you detect a viewpoint or bias in any of the text of the site? What is it?

_____

_____

_____

_____

_____

_____

_____

COVERAGE

1. Why would you visit this site? Do you want to purchase something, visit someplace, enroll in a program, or become a member of an organization? Do you want to know about employment opportunities?

_____

_____

_____

_____

_____

_____

_____

2. Form some questions (for example, Is the Los Angeles Police Department currently hiring? What are the winter hours at Yellowstone National Park? Can I order a refrigerator online from Sears?). Then, test the site for its ability to answer your questions.

_____

_____

_____

_____

_____

_____

STABILITY

1. When was this site created and when was it updated?

_____

_____

_____

_____

_____

_____

2. Are the links still in existence?

_____

_____

_____

_____

_____

_____

_____

_____

3. Email the contact person for the site. Did you get a reply? Was the message deliverable?

_____

_____

_____

_____

_____

_____

_____

Chapter 15 | Using and Evaluating Internet Sources

Exercise E   15d Evaluating Internet Sites

Visit the Web site for any college or university of your choice. Attempt the following activities and share your responses with your classmates. Explain how many steps you had to take to get the information.

1. Locate the online college catalog. What did you have to do to find it? How many steps were involved? How many false starts?

_____

_____

_____

_____

_____

_____

_____

_____

2. Locate the U.S. mail address and phone number for the college or university. Where did you find it? How many steps did it take?

_____

_____

_____

_____

_____

_____

_____

_____

3. Locate the academic department of your choice. Can you find a list of faculty in that department? Is there contact information, such as office location, phone number, and email address? Are photographs included?

_____

_____

_____

_____

_____

_____

_____

4. Locate the map of the campus. Can you locate specific buildings? Can you locate parking? If you were a first-time visitor to the campus, could you find the Admissions Office or the Registrar? Can you locate a desk or place to get information?

_____

_____

_____

_____

_____

_____

_____

_____

5. What are the entrance requirements for this college or university? Where did you find them? How many steps were involved?

_____

_____

_____

_____

_____

_____

6. Once you share these responses in class, share the "best" and "worst" experiences in locating the information.

_____

_____

_____

_____

_____

_____

EXTRA ACTIVITY

Email the Webmaster of the Web site and let your successes and concerns be known. If any of this basic information was difficult to access, the college should be told.

Chapter 16 Summarizing, Paraphrasing, Quoting, and Synthesizing Sources

Exercise A   16a Writing a Summary

Either select a text from the reader you currently use in your English class or go to the Web site for Project Gutenberg at www.gutenberg.net to locate a text for summarizing. This site includes hundreds of works that are in the public domain. If you are looking for nonfiction essays, try searching by an author's name. Some good authors to try are Ralph Waldo Emerson, Henry David Thoreau, Nathaniel Hawthorne, William and Henry James, Sigmund Freud, William Dean Howells, Mark Twain (Samuel Clemens), and T. S. Eliot. Try to locate an essay that is about five to ten pages long.

Because you can download these texts, you can make electronic notations or print the text of your choice. Your instructor may select a specific work for the class or for group work as well. First, read and annotate your source text. Then, using the criteria in Chapter 16a and the following directions, prepare a summary of 100 to 250 words. Take particular care when you write the first sentence; assume that your reader needs the work and author identified.

1. Your opening sentence should, first of all, identify the *author* and *title* of the work you are about to summarize. Be sure to punctuate the title correctly (see section 57a).

2. Next, your opening sentence should identify the basic *structure* of the essay you read. A good place for structure words is the verb of your sentence; for example, the author "argues" or "classifies" would indicate structure.

3. Third, your opening sentence should suggest the *tone* of the essay.

4. Finally, the statement should express the main idea or *thesis* of the essay. Remember, a thesis is more than just naming the topic or subject matter. You need to state the thesis in your own words—not the *author's* words.

5. After you have prepared the opening statement, your summary should consist of concise, well-worded sentences stating only the *main* points of the work being summarized.

6. Avoid direct quotations in a summary because quotations are not concise. However, if exact wording is essential to understanding, use quotations, properly documented, with discretion.

_____

_____

_____

_____

_____

_____

_____

_____

_____

_____

_____

_____

_____

_____

_____

_____

_____

_____

_____

Chapter 16	Summarizing, Paraphrasing, Quoting, and Synthesizing Sources

Exercise B   16b Writing a Paraphrase

Using the same reading selection you summarized in Exercise A, select particular passages to paraphrase. Cut and paste the passage you are paraphrasing; be sure to place it in quotation marks and document it. Then prepare a paraphrase on the same page. Share these examples in peer groups or in a whole-class activity. Documents may be projected or shared online as well.

Evaluate the effectiveness of the paraphrase based on the criteria in Chapter 15. Use the following checklist and suggest revisions if the paraphrase does not meet the criteria.

☐ Is the paraphrase original? Do any passages use original source language and/or structure?

☐ Is the paraphrase accurate? Does it reflect the views of the source?

☐ Is the paraphrase objective? Does it stick entirely with the source author's views?

☐ Is the paraphrase complete? Has it kept or omitted any important ideas?

Chapter 16	Summarizing, Paraphrasing, Quoting, and Synthesizing Sources

Exercise C   16c–d Quoting and Integrating Sources

Return to the work you selected in Exercise A. Select key words and phrases that would be useful to quote in a longer paper. Review the Checklist: When to Quote from Chapter 16c for making choices. Expand your summary into an essay of 500 to 750 words, incorporating selected quotes in the body paragraphs. Use the quotations only for support—not as attention devices—for this paper. Integrate the quotations with identifying tags. *Hint:* Watch out for sentences starting with "This" after the quotation. You may have created a pronoun reference error (see section 47c).

_____

_____

_____

_____

_____

_____

_____

_____

_____

_____

_____

_____

_____

_____

_____

_____

| Chapter 16 | Summarizing, Paraphrasing, Quoting, and Synthesizing Sources |

Exercise D   16d Synthesizing Sources

Read the following two paragraphs, which lack supporting quotations. After each paragraph is a selection of possible quotations. Choose the best supporting quotation and determine where it should be placed in the paragraph. If more than one quote is suitable, discuss why you made the choices you did. Add a voice tag, edit the quotation, or include other wording for better paragraph coherence.

EXAMPLE 1

While slavery was a terrible oppression and violation of human rights in the pre–Civil War South, women slaves bore the double burden of sexual oppression as well. In Harriet A. Jacobs's *Incidents in the Life of a Slave Girl*, she recounts her escape and subsequent life in hiding after her master attempted to rape her. She hid for seven years in an attic garret measuring seven by nine feet, with the highest part being only three feet. She hid to be near her beloved children, but she suffered frostbite in winter, sweltering heat in summer, and crippling physical damage due to the cramped quarters. At the end of seven years, Jacobs survived to write of her experiences.

Quote 1: "The rats and mice ran over my bed."

Quote 2: "But though my life in slavery was comparatively devoid of hardships God pity the woman who is compelled to lead such a life!"

Quote 3: "Often I was obliged to lie in bed all day to keep comfortable; but with all my precautions, my shoulders and feet were frostbitten."

Source of quotations: Harriet Jacobs. *Incidents in the Life of a Slave Girl.* Mineola, NY: Dover Publications, 2001.

EXAMPLE 2

Most non-Chinese Americans believe they understand the Chinese culture through Chinese food that is an American invention or the famous Chinatowns of cities such as San Francisco, which exist primarily to attract tourists. Lack of knowledge of the cultural heritage of Chinese Americans has led to stereotypes. These stereo-types have been promoted through film images and confusion among the general population about the distinct traits of various Asian ethnicities. As Shawn Wong, noted Chinese author, points out, after the bombing of Pearl Harbor, Chinese Americans wore buttons reading "I am Chinese" (Wong 1).

Quote 1: "Depending on our level of acceptance or rejection, the Chinese in America migrated from yellow peril to World War II ally to red scare to model minority."

Quote 2: "And on a personal level, each Asian American struggles against a media identity that is not entirely true."

Quote 3: "Indeed, some Chinese American historians and sociolo-gists have even encouraged invisibility."

Source of quotations: Shawn Wong. *Asian American Literature: A Brief Introduction and Anthology.* Upper Saddle River, NJ: Pearson Education, 1997, preface.

Chapter 17 | Avoid Plagiarism

Exercise A | 17c Revising to Eliminate Plagiarism

In each of the plagiarized passages below the writer has committed one or more errors identified in Chapter 17c of your handbook. For each passage, identify the error type(s) and possible correction(s) and write the corresponding letter(s) from the following choices beside the passage.

A. Enclose borrowed words in quotation marks.

B. Do not imitate a source's syntax and phrasing.

C. Document statistics obtained from a source.

D. Differentiate your words and ideas from those of the source.

EXAMPLE 1

Original: "Underlying the suggestions [defending the English Department at the University of Nairobi, Kenya] is a basic assumption that the English tradition and the emergence of the modern west is the central root of our consciousness and cultural heritage. Africa becomes an extension of the west, an attitude which, until radical reassessment, used to dictate the teaching and organization of History in our University. [. . .] Here then, is our main question: If there is need for a 'study of the historic continuity of a single culture', why can't this be African? Why can't African literature be at the centre so that we can view other cultures in relationship to it?"

Source: Ngugi Wa Thiong'o, Taban Lo Liyon, and Henry Owuor-Anyumba, "On the Abolition of the English Department." From *Homecoming: Essays on African and Caribbean Literature, Culture and Politics.* London: Heinemann Educational Books, 1972.

Plagiarism: Teaching English in a major African university is the central root of our consciousness and cultural heritage. African literature needs to be at the center of study because otherwise Africa becomes an extension of the West. Other cultures should be viewed in relation to Africa instead.

EXAMPLE 2

Original: "The Orient is not only adjacent to Europe; it is also the place of Europe's greatest and richest and oldest colonies, the source of its civilizations and languages, its cultural contestant, and one of its deepest and most recurring images of the Other. In addition, the

99

Orient has helped to define Europe (or the West) as its contrasting image, idea, personality, experience. Yet none of this Orient is merely imaginative. The Orient is an integral part of European *material* civilization and culture."

Source: Edward Said. *Orientalism*. New York: Random House, 1978.

Plagiarism: The Orient provides three things for Europe: its civilizations and languages, its culture, and its images of something apart from the European. Europe is the opposite of the Orient. Contrast is part of defining identity.

EXAMPLE 3

Original: "History teaches us clearly that the battle against colonialism does not run straight away along the lines of nationalism. For a very long time the native devotes his energies to ending certain definite abuses: forced labor, corporal punishment, inequality of salaries, limitation of political rights, etc. This fight for democracy against the oppression of mankind will slowly leave the confusion of neo-liberal universalism to emerge, sometimes laboriously, as a claim to nationhood. It so happens that the unpreparedness of the educated classes, the lack of practical links between them and the mass of the people, their laziness, and, let it be said, their cowardice at the decisive moment of the struggle will give rise to tragic mishaps."

Source: Frantz Fanon. *The Wretched of the Earth*. Trans. Constance Farrington. New York: Grove Press, 1986.

Plagiarism: Frantz Fanon claims that countries newly freed from colonial rule are in big trouble because the educated classes are underprepared and the working classes are disconnected, lazy, and afraid. The natives spent most of their energies fighting forced labor, physical abuse, low pay, and restricted rights.

Chapter 18 MLA Documentation Style

Exercise A 18a Using MLA Style

You are writing a research paper on Bram Stoker's *Dracula* and have located the novel and a variety of secondary sources from your college online catalog and several periodical databases. You have acquired the original print version of the Hustis article, but you are using the database version of the Halberstam article. You have sent for the unpublished doctoral dissertation. Turn the information into bibliographic citations in correct MLA style and alphabetize the list as you would for your Works Cited.

1. Book 1:

   Author: Joseph Valente

   Title: *Dracula's crypt: Bram Stoker, Irishness, and the question of blood*

   Place of publication: Urbana, Illinois

   Publisher: University of Illinois Press

   Date of publication: 2002

2. Book 2:

   Author: Bram Stoker

   Title: *Dracula*

   Place of publication: New York

   Publisher: TOR

   Date of publication: 1997

3. Book 3:

   Author: Donald F. Glut

   Title: *The Dracula Book*

Place of publication: Metuchen, New Jersey

Publisher: Scarecrow Press

Date of publication: 1975

4. Article 1:

Author: Harriet Hustis

Article title: Black and White and Read All Over: Performative Textuality in Bram Stoker's Dracula

Magazine/journal: *Studies in the Novel*

Volume: 33

Issue: none

Date: spring 2001

Pages: 18

5. Article 2:

Author: Judith Halberstam

Article title: Technologies of monstrosity: Bram Stoker's 'Dracula'

Magazine/journal: *Victorian Studies*

Volume: 36

Issue: 3

Date: spring 1993

Pages: 333 (20)

Database: Infotrac Expanded Academic ASAP

6. Unpublished Doctoral Dissertation:

Author: Lenora P. Ledwon

Title: Legal fictions: constructions of the female legal subject in nineteenth-century law and literature

University: University of Notre Dame

Date: 1993

Chapter 19	APA Documentation Style

Exercise A — 19a Using APA Style

You are writing a research paper on the incidence of smallpox among native populations of North and Central America after they came into contact with the Europeans. You have the following list of sources. Convert the information into a reference list in APA style.

1. Book:

   Author: Jonathan B. Tucker

   Title: Scourge: the once and future threat of smallpox

   Place of publication: New York

   Publisher: Atlantic Monthly Press

   Date of publication: 2001

2. Article in print form:

   Author: Geoffrey Cowley

   Title: The great disease migration

   Magazine/journal: *Newsweek*

   Date: fall-winter 1991

   Volume: 118

   Page: 54 (3)

3. Article in print form:

   Author: Thomas H. Brown

   Title: The African connection; Cotton Mather and the Boston smallpox

   Magazine/journal: *JAMA, The Journal of the American Medical Association*

Volume: 260

Number: 15

Date: Oct. 21, 1988

Page: 2247 (3)

4. Article from database:

Author: Derrick Baxby

Title: The end of smallpox

Magazine/journal: *History Today*

Volume: 49

Number: 3

Date: March 1999

Page: 14 (1)

Chapter 20 | Chicago Documentation Style

Exercise A | 20a Using Chicago Style

As part of an American history course, you have just viewed Steven Spielberg's film from 1998 entitled *Amistad*. You have noted some of the characters and settings and are putting together a list of bibliographic citations in Chicago documentation style. You're interested in the political careers of John Quincy Adams, Martin Van Buren, and John Calhoun. You also want to know more about the Mende people, the Lomboko Slave Fortress, and Sierra Leone. You have the following information. Convert it into a bibliography in Chicago style. For additional sources, do a subject search on your library's databases and add to this list of references.

1. Movie:

   Director: Steven Spielberg

   Title: *Amistad*

   Date: 1998

   Production company: Dreamworks

2. Book:

   Editors: John A. Williams and Charles F. Harris

   Title: *Amistad 1*

   Place of publication: New York

   Publisher: Random House

   Date of publication: 1970

3. Anonymous Web site:

   Title: The movie

   Web address: http://home.sandiego.edu/~escott/movie.html

4. Online article:

   Author: Bina Williams

Article: Famous American Trials: Amistad Trials 1839–1840

Magazine/journal: *School Library Journal*

Date: July 2003

Volume: 49

Issue: 7

Page: 56

Chapter 21	**CSE and Other Documentation Styles**

Exercise A	**21a Using CSE Style**

You have just learned of a rare genetic disease called *cystinosis*. You need to locate current information, so you have searched databases and Web sites and have come up with the following items. Turn them into a CSE citation-sequence reference list.

1. Web site:

   Title: Cystinosis Central

   Author: University of California, San Diego, Department of Pediatrics, Division of Metabolic Disease

   Web address: http://medicine.ucsd.edu/cystinosis/INDEX.htm

2. Online article:

   Authors: E.T. Tsilou, D. Thompson, A.S. Lindblad, G.F. Reed, B. Rubin, W. Gahl, J. Thoene, M. Del Monte, J.A. Schneider, D.B. Granet, M.I. Kaiser-Kupfer

   Title: A multicentre randomized double-masked clinical trial of a new formulation of topical cysteamine for the treatment of corneal cystine crystals in cystinosis.

   Journal: *British Journal of Ophthalmology*

   Date: January 2003

   Volume: 87

   Issue: 1

   Page: 28 (4)

3. Print article:

   Authors: A. Helip Wooley, J. Thoene

   Title: Tissue-specific expression and regulation of CTNS

Journal: *American Journal of Human Genetics*

Date: October 2001

Volume: 69

Issue: 4

Page: 483

| Chapter 22 | **Writing in the Humanities** |

Exercise A   22b Response Essay

Review section 22b of your handbook for writing a response essay. Then, visit an art museum, do a Web search for a work of art that interests you, or use a search engine to locate one of the sites listed below. Note that the Web sites for some of the museums are not in English, but none of them is too difficult to navigate. Select one work of visual art that you can see firsthand or that is clearly reproduced on a Web site. Jot down your responses as you view it.

SUGGESTED WEB SITES

The Metropolitan Museum of Art, New York City

The Art Institute of Chicago

The National American Art Museum of the Smithsonian, Washington, DC

The Vatican Museums, Vatican City

The Prado, Madrid, Spain

The Sofia Reina National Museum, Madrid, Spain

The Uffizi, Florence, Italy

_____

_____

_____

_____

_____

_____

_____

_____

_____

_____

_____

CHECKLIST

☐ Did you clearly identify the name of the work, the artist, the type of work, and the medium used?

☐ Did you identify the location of the work and the manner in which you viewed it?

☐ Did you write a very brief historical and cultural context for the work?

☐ Did you give a very brief summary of the work's distinguishing characteristics?

☐ Are you writing your responses in the first person?

☐ If you actually visited a museum, how did the overall environment, and even the people, influence your experience?

☐ If you viewed the work on a Web site, how does this experience differ from an actual visit to the work?

Chapter 22 | Writing in the Humanities

Exercise B | 22b Annotated Bibliography

Return to the citations you prepared for Exercise A in Chapter 18. If you did not do that exercise, prepare the citations and locate the articles identified there, or locate additional articles on the topic of Bram Stoker's *Dracula*. Select three to five articles, read them, and prepare annotations.

CRITERIA

- Limit your annotations to about 100 words unless your instructor states otherwise.
- Summarize the article concisely and completely.
- What information and insights are gained from each article?
- Evaluate its usefulness for your upcoming research paper.

Chapter 22 | Writing in the Humanities

Exercise C | 22f Research Sources

Your handbook supplies a list of reference books in the humanities in section 22f. Access your college's online catalog and find out how many of these reference works are in your library. You may want to do this activity as a group exercise and divide the categories of reference works among people.

Generally, reference works do not circulate and cannot be borrowed through the interlibrary loan system. Answer the following questions about these works.

1. Where can you find these works physically in your college library?

_____

_____

_____

2. How are they cataloged? Is the call number distinct in any way?

_____

_____

_____

3. Do all the books fit on standard-size shelves?

_____

_____

_____

4. Which references are single-volume works? Which are multivolume?

_____

_____

_____

_____

_____

_____

_____

5. Select the available works in one category. How often are they updated? What is the date on the most recent volume you have located?

_____

_____

_____

_____

_____

_____

Chapter 23 | Writing a Literary Analysis

Exercise A   **23c Sample Literary Analysis (without Sources)**

Read the following Shakespearean sonnet. Then answer the questions that follow in anticipation of writing your own literary analysis. You may also apply these questions to any poem of your choice.

SONNET #9

Is it for fear to wet a widow's eye
That thou consum'st thyself in single life?
Ah, if thou issueless shalt hap to die,
The world will wail thee like a makeless wife.
The world will be thy widow, and still weep
That thou no form of thee hast left behind,
When every private widow well may keep
By children's eyes her husband's shape in mind.
Look what an unthrift in the world doth spend
Shifts but his place, for still the world enjoys it;
But beauty's waste that in the world an end,
And kept unused, the user so destroys it.
      No love toward others in that bosom sits
      That on himself such murd'rous shame commits.

1. Read the poem out loud. Before attempting to paraphrase it, check the language to make sure you understand the words. Some of the words may be archaic, so discuss or research meanings.
   a. Explain some of the verb forms: *consum'st, shalt, hap, hast*
   b. Check the meanings of *issueless, makeless, unthrift*

2. This poem is a Shakespearean or English sonnet. Identify the characteristics of this type of sonnet.
   a. How many lines does the poem have?
   b. What is the rhyme pattern?
   c. What is the metrical pattern?

3. The voice of the poem is the speaker. What can you tell about the speaker? Is someone also being addressed? What is the issue with the listener?

4. Paraphrase the sonnet in sections. The logic of the English sonnet is to develop the ideas in four quatrains (four-line units) and a final couplet. Shakespeare punctuates each of these sections with a period, so he completes a sentence.
   a. The first quatrain (lines 1–4) contains a question and an answer. What is the speaker asking?
   b. In the second quatrain (lines 5–8), the speaker says that "the world will be thy widow." Why? What does he mean by this metaphor?
   c. What will happen to the listener's beauty in the third quatrain (lines 9–12)?
   d. The final couple sums up the point the speaker has been developing. What is the message for the listener?

5. Expand on the theme of love as it is expressed in this sonnet. What is said about love? What is the connection to the "single life" (line 2) and being "issueless" (line 3)?

Chapter 24	**Writing a Literary Argument**

Exercise A   24a Planning a Literary Argument

Examine the following statements that are proposed as thesis statements for a literary argument. Discuss whether or not they are arguable and focused. If they are a statement of fact or a broad generality, then label them accordingly.

> F = Statement of fact
>
> G = Generality
>
> AT = Arguable thesis

_____ 1. In *Wuthering Heights*, Heathcliff is adopted into the Earnshaw household.

_____ 2. In *Wuthering Heights*, Heathcliff's cruelty is a result of the treatment he receives from the Earnshaw children.

_____ 3. In *Wuthering Heights*, the Earnshaw family is completely dysfunctional.

_____ 4. The Shakespearean or English sonnet consists of fourteen lines organized in three quatrains and a final rhymed couplet.

_____ 5. The Shakespearean or English sonnet and the Petrarchan or Italian sonnet differ in the rhyme patterns and overall structure.

_____ 6. The central irony of Yasmina Khadra's novel, *The Swallows of Kabul*, is that the burqa denies and obliterates a woman's identity but also allows one woman to save another's life for that very reason.

_____ 7. In Yasmina Khadra's novel, *The Swallows of Kabul*, life in Afghanistan under the Taliban is harsh.

_____ 8. In Caryl Churchill's play, *Top Girls*, the first act portrays women from different historical periods meeting for a dinner party.

_____ 9. In Caryl Churchill's play, *Top Girls*, Lady Nijo reveals herself as a victim of cultural restrictions on women.

_____10. In the Harry Potter series of novels, Hermione, Ron Weasly, and Harry are allegorical figures of Wisdom, Heart or Compassion, and Courage.

Name _____ Date _____ Score _____

| Chapter 25 | **Writing in the Social Sciences** |

| **Exercise A** | **25b Writing Assignments** |

You have been required to read Leonard L. Berry's book, *Discovering the Soul of Service* (The Free Press: Simon & Schuster, 1999), for one of your classes. The following is a series of writing assignments based on the companies he has highlighted for their quality service in his book. All but the second assignment can be completed without reading the book. Use the guidelines for writing assignments in your handbook, section 25b.

1. **Personal Experience Essay:** Visit a store or office for one of the businesses Berry lists in the back of his book (pp. 257–260) and write a personal experience essay. These companies have many sites, so you should be able to find a store or office easily. They are listed here in case you do not have access to the book.

Bergstrom Hotels

The Charles Schwab Corporation

Chick-fil-A

The Container Store

GfK Custom Research Inc.

Dana Commercial Credit Corporation

Dial-A-Mattress

Enterprise rent-a-car

Midwest Express Airlines

Miller SQA

Special Expeditions

St. Paul Saints

Ukrop's Super Markets

USAA

2. **Book Review:** Following the guidelines in 24b, prepare a book review of Berry's book.

3. **Case Study:** Use one of the businesses listed here and prepare a formal case study of the company and its quality management practices.

4. **Annotated Bibliography and Review-of-Research Essay:** Locate three to five articles on the company you selected and prepare an annotated bibliography. Develop a review-of-research essay using the annotations.

5. **Proposal:** Prepare a proposal for an extended research project on the company of your choice.

Chapter 25 Writing in the Social Sciences

Exercise B   25f Research Sources

Your handbook supplies a list of reference books in the social sciences in section 25f. Access your college's online catalog and find out how many of the reference works are in your library. You may want to do this activity as a group exercise and divide the categories of reference works among people.

Generally, reference works do not circulate and cannot be borrowed through the interlibrary loan system. Answer the following questions about these works.

1. Where do you find these works physically in your college library?

_____

_____

_____

2. How are they cataloged? Is the call number distinct in any way?

_____

_____

_____

3. Do all the books fit on standard-size shelves?

_____

_____

_____

4. Which references are single-volume works? Which are multivolume?

_____

_____

_____

_____

_____

_____

_____

5. Select the available works in one category. How often are they updated? What is the date on the most recent volume you have located?

_____

_____

_____

_____

_____

_____

_____

Chapter 26	**Writing in the Natural and Applied Sciences**

Exercise A   26b Writing Assignments

Section 26b of the handbook discusses abstracts. In Exercise A for Chapter 21, you researched the rare genetic disease called cystinosis and prepared CSEstyle citations for several articles. Access these articles, or others on the same topic, on the Web and write abstracts for the articles.

When you do online research for periodical articles, notice that many databases supply abstracts alone and also articles with abstracts. Locate several articles with abstracts and compare the professional abstracts with the articles by answering the following questions.

1. Are these abstracts *indicative* or *informative*?

   _____

   _____

   _____

2. How long are the professional abstracts?

   _____

   _____

   _____

3. Can you identify the purpose, methodology, results, and conclusions of the articles in their abstracts?

   _____

   _____

   _____

   _____

   _____

   _____

Chapter 26 | Writing in the Natural and Applied Sciences

Exercise B | 26f Research Sources

Your handbook supplies a list of reference books in the natural and applied sciences in section 26f. Access your college's online catalog and find out how many of these reference works are in its library. You may want to do this activity as a group exercise and divide the categories of reference works among people.

Generally, reference works do not circulate and cannot be borrowed through the interlibrary loan system. Answer the following questions about these works.

1. Where can you find these works physically in your college library?

_____

_____

_____

2. How are they catalogued? Is the call number distinct in any way?

_____

_____

_____

3. Do all the books fit on standard-size shelves?

_____

_____

_____

4. Which references are single-volume works? Which are multivolume?

_____

_____

_____

_____

_____

_____

_____

5. Select the available works in one category. How often are they updated? What is the date on the most recent volume you have located?

_____

_____

_____

_____

_____

_____

_____

Chapter 27   Ten Habits of Successful Students

Exercise A   **27b Put Studying First**

Do you know your learning style? You may wish to investigate this topic. To learn more, locate the sources listed below. You may be able to check out Dunn, Dunn, and Price's *Learning Styles Inventory.* Consult a counselor or trained professional at your college to pursue the issue.

Dunn, R., and Dunn, K. (1992). *Teaching elementary students through their individual learning styles.* Needham Heights, MA: Allyn & Bacon.

Dunn, R., Dunn, K., and Price, G. E. (2000). *Learning Styles Inventory.* Lawrence, KS: Price Systems.

Hill, J. (1971). *Personalized education programs utilizing cognitive style mapping.* Bloomfield Hills, MI: Oakland Community College.

Keefe, J. W. (1991). *Learning style: Cognitive and thinking skills.* Reston, VA: National Association of Secondary School Principals.

Chapter 27 | Ten Habits of Successful Students

Exercise B   **27f–h Take Advantage of College Services,
Use the Library, and Use Technology**

Go to your college's Web site. Then, answer the following questions.

1. Can you locate a map of the physical layout of the campus or campuses? Are street addresses provided if multiple buildings exist?

_____

2. Does the first page indicate the services a first-time student would need? Can you find admissions, registration, and counseling easily?

_____

3. Does your college have online registration? Online counseling and advising? Touchtone registration?

_____

4. Can you access the college catalog easily?

_____

5. Can you locate contact information for instructors? Are both full-time and part-time instructors listed? Are pictures included? Can you link directly to each one's email? Do instructors have personal Web pages?

_____

_____

6. Can you locate hours or schedules for computer labs? Tutoring or writing centers? Workout facilities? The bookstore? The health center? Can you contact these places by phone and email?

_____

_____

7. Does your library have an online catalog? Can it be accessed if you are off campus? Can the various databases be accessed off campus? Can you email information to yourself?

_____

_____

8. How do you get your student ID and email account? Is getting them automatic when you enroll? How do you get your password?

_____

_____

9. Do your instructors use computer technology, such as Blackboard or WebCT, to post information about courses? Are you expected to access this information as part of your course requirements?

_____

_____

Name _____ Date _____ Score _____

| Chapter 27 | **Ten Habits of Successful Students** |

Exercise C   **Student Self-Assessment**

The following tables can help with a self-assessment of your habits. Complete the tables once at the beginning of the semester and again toward the end.

Use the rating system provided and circle a number for each item. Then take a hard look at your scores. Consistent ratings of 5 are a measure of high-quality management of work habits. Frequent ratings of 1, 2, or 3 indicate areas in need of serious work. Don't just settle for a rating of 4—push yourself to do better!

Rating System: 1 = never, 2 = rarely, 3 = some of the time, 4 = most of the time, 5 = always

Attendance and Promptness					
I attend class.	1	2	3	4	5
I come to class on time.	1	2	3	4	5
I stay until the end of class.	1	2	3	4	5

Active Preparation					
I spend two hours on preparation for each hour of class time.	1	2	3	4	5
I am caught up on my reading assignments.	1	2	3	4	5
I prepare for each class by reading assigned materials.	1	2	3	4	5
I prepare for each class by making notes.	1	2	3	4	5
I prepare for each class by annotating text.	1	2	3	4	5
I prepare for each class by looking up words I don't understand.	1	2	3	4	5
I prepare for each class by completing written homework.	1	2	3	4	5
I have written homework prepared on time.	1	2	3	4	5
I set high goals for myself in meeting class requirements.	1	2	3	4	5

Active Participation and Courtesy

I participate in class discussions.	1	2	3	4	5
I participate in group activities.	1	2	3	4	5
I contribute thoughtfully during class discussions.	1	2	3	4	5
I contribute thoughtfully durng group activities.	1	2	3	4	5
I am polite and respectful to my instructor.	1	2	3	4	5
I am polite and respectful to fellow students.	1	2	3	4	5
I listen attentively to everyone else's contributions.	1	2	3	4	5

Using Resources Effectively

If I have questions in class, I ask them.	1	2	3	4	5
When I feel I need help, I seek out my instructor.	1	2	3	4	5
When I feel I need help, I seek out services such as tutoring.	1	2	3	4	5
When I feel I need help, I ask fellow students.	1	2	3	4	5
I know where resources for tutoring and support are located.	1	2	3	4	5

Intellectual Honesty

I understand the meaning of plagiarism.	1	2	3	4	5
I understand why plagiarism is wrong.	1	2	3	4	5
I do my own schoolwork.	1	2	3	4	5
When I research materials, I keep a record of references to cite.	1	2	3	4	5
I understand and appreciate the value of originality.	1	2	3	4	5

Chapter 28 Writing Essay Exams

Exercise A   28a Planning an Essay Exam Answer

Review the Close-up: Key Words in Exam Questions in Chapter 28a of your handbook. Examine the following essay exam questions and underline the key words. Then, answer the following questions; be sure to consider issues of both completeness and correctness in your answers: What would be the minimum requirements for a correct answer to each question? Why might you lose points when answering?

1. Identify three distinguishing characteristics of French Impressionist art. Select one artist of that movement and explain how he or she applies the characteristics.

   _____

   _____

   _____

   _____

   _____

   _____

2. In the "Wife of Bath's Tale" from Geoffrey Chaucer's *Canterbury Tales*, the old woman lectures the young knight on *gentilesse*. What is the meaning of this term, and why is it important for the young knight to learn and practice its true meaning?

   _____

   _____

   _____

   _____

   _____

   _____

3. Barbara Tuchman explains that the Black Plague during the fourteenth century actually had some social benefits for the survivors. Identify three of the benefits and explain why they were a result of the plague.

_____

_____

_____

_____

_____

_____

4. What was the importance of Delphi in ancient Greece? What does *omphalos* mean, and why is this term important to Delphi? How did the oracle function in ancient Delphi, and how did she contribute to the importance of the site?

_____

_____

_____

_____

_____

_____

5. Compare and contrast the theories of human behavior of Sigmund Freud and B. F. Skinner.

_____

_____

_____

_____

_____

_____

6. Trace the origins and differences in form between the Italian or Petrarchan sonnet and the English or Shakespearean sonnet.

_____

_____

_____

_____

_____

_____

7. What was the Royal Society? What were its origins, and who were the society's early members? Identify one important member and explain in detail the reason this person was invited to join.

_____

_____

_____

_____

_____

_____

8. Who was King Kamehameha? Why was he important?

_____

_____

_____

_____

_____

_____

9. What are the characteristics of Hansen's disease? What was its former name?

_____

_____

_____

_____

_____

_____

10. On the Sistine Chapel's ceiling, Michelangelo alternated figures of Biblical prophets and ancient sibyls. Compare and contrast a prophet and a sibyl. Identify one of each by name, and explain the particular importance of that prophet and that sibyl.

_____

_____

_____

_____

_____

Chapter 28 | Writing Essay Exams

Exercise B   28b Shaping an Essay Exam Answer

For this activity, work in either pairs or small groups. Select one question from Exercise A for Chapter 28. Create an effective thesis statement. Check it for focus, completeness, and relevance to the question.

_____

_____

_____

_____

_____

_____

_____

_____

_____

_____

_____

_____

_____

_____

_____

Chapter 28 | Writing Essay Exams

Exercise C | 28d Writing Paragraph-Length Essay Exam Answers

One common type of paragraph-length essay exam question is the formal definition and illustration structure. Individually or in groups, select one or more of the terms in the list below and prepare a paragraph-length formal definition and illustration. Review Chapter 7d on definition as a pattern.

TERMS

serendipity

gentilesse
(Middle English)

angst

hubris

epiphany

DNA

eurocentrism

aborigine

nuclear fission

antiphon

quid pro quo

deus ex machina

annulment

paradox

tsunami

_____

_____

_____

_____

_____

_____

_____

_____

_____

_____

_____

Chapter 29 | Writing for the Workplace

Exercise A | 29a Writing Letters of Application

Do a Web search for a position that meets your current qualifications. Examine www.monster.com and the classified ads for an online newspaper in your area. Following the guidelines in your handbook, Chapter 29, prepare a letter of application. Then check the letter by answering the following questions. You may choose to check the letter individually, in pairs, or in small groups.

FORMAT

1. Is the layout visually appealing? Have you centered the letter both vertically and horizontally? Have you provided adequate white space?

2. Have you selected a font style and size that is easy to read?

3. Have you chosen a known layout style: full block, modified block, or indented? Have you remained consistent in this style?

4. Are each of the required parts of a letter included: heading with date, inside address, greeting, body paragraphs, complimentary close, and signature block?

5. Have you avoided any temptations to be gimmicky with font and layout?

CONTENT

1. Does the first paragraph identify the source of your information? Does it identify the exact position title? Is your tone professional?

2. Have you explained your distinctive qualifications for the position? Have you provided more information than a recap of your resume?

3. Have you used a persuasive and enthusiastic tone throughout the letter? Have you avoided jargon and wordiness? Have you been honest and accurate with your information?

4. Have you closed the letter with exact contact information: phone numbers, email address, or other pertinent information?

Name _____ Date _____ Score _____

Exercise B | **29d Writing Memos**

Write one of the following using either one of the memo templates in your word-processing program or a memo format design of your own.

1. Write a pair of memoranda, one from a supervisor to a specific employee and one a reply from the employee to the supervisor, or vice versa. The content should specify an assignment the supervisor is making and an employee's report on its status, or a request by the employee for directions on a project, in addition to a response from the supervisor.

2. Write a memorandum from a supervisor to a group of employees concerning either a new or changed work policy, an announcement of a new training program, or an announcement of a special meeting. Include all relevant facts, such as the date, place, and purpose.

3. As a supervisor, write a memorandum to employees, which is to be posted, concerning a new policy or procedure at work. Some suggestions to consider: a policy on the use of a machine (for example, copy machine or fax), a guideline on workplace visits and phone calls from friends or relatives, or a warning about personal emails and Web-surfing during working hours. Another type of memorandum could be one to post that is to be read by the public (for example, visitors to a hospital).

Name _____ Date _____ Score _____

Exercise A 30d Using Visuals

Convert the following information into tables with appropriate headings and descriptive captions. See Chapter 30d in your handbook for an example.

1. Registration for spring semester will begin on October 15. Students who have earned 90 credit hours or more have priority for registration, October 15–17. Students with 60 to 89 hours can register October 18–20. Students with 30 to 59 hours can register from October 21–23. Beginning October 24, all students can register. Registration ends January 4.

2. Students planning to take English courses must first take a placement exam. They can take the ASSET reading and writing tests, the COMPASS reading and writing tests, or the Macon College writing sample. The ASSET tests will be given on March 3 from 8:00 A.M. to 12:00 noon at Prairie High School, March 15 from 1:00 to 5:00 P.M. at Macon College, and March 21 from 6:00 to 10:00 P.M. at Dover Community College. The COMPASS tests can be taken Monday through Saturday beginning March 1 from 8:00 A.M. to 4:00 P.M. at the Dover Community College Learning Center. The Macon College writing sample will be offered only on March 26 from 8:00 A.M. to 10:00 A.M. and again from 12 noon to 2:00 P.M. in the Macon College Learning Center.

Chapter 31 | Designing Web Sites

Exercise A | 31a–g Designing Web Sites

Using the guidelines and the checklists in Chapter 31 of your handbook, create a Web site for your English class if you have access to a relatively easy-to-use Web authoring software. Here are the steps to use.

1. As a whole class, decide on your purpose, audience, and tone (see section 31a).

2. As a whole class, brainstorm and create either an informal outline or a storyboard (see section 31a).

3. Form groups for the following tasks:
   - Visuals group: This group will select graphics and take appropriate pictures (see section 31c). Photographs of the class in action or of smaller groups at work would be good.
   - Text group: This group will write the text.
   - Navigation group: This group will plan the navigation (see section 31d) for the site.

4. Test the Web site by logging on and using it. Fine-tune any flaws or confusing navigation spots. Edit any errors in text. Improve the size and layout of visuals as needed.

Chapter 32   Making Oral Presentations

Exercise A   32d Preparing Visual Aids

Choosing the most suitable visuals for an oral presentation is a challenging task. An elaborate presentation that depends on sophisticated technology may contain obstacles because of some failure of the technology. Visuals that do not take the size of the room and sight lines into account will not convey your message to the audience. Certain types of visuals are just more suited to specific speaking situations.

A list of visuals and their main functions is provided. Read the speaking situations described below and suggest the most suitable visuals by inserting the letter corresponding to a type of visual beside the numbered situation. Several different visuals can be used in any one situation. You should also indicate which delivery method you plan to use: computer presentation, physical materials, or handouts. If you have the capability, prepare a visual for each speaking situation. This project can be done individually or in groups.

SELECTING VISUALS

A. Illustrating numerical information—tables and graphs (bar, line, pie chart, pictograph)

B. Illustrating logical relationships—diagrams, organizational charts

C. Illustrating processes and instructions—checklists, tables, flowcharts, logic boxes and trees, objects

D. Illustrating objects and spatial traits—photographs, drawings, maps, screen shots, objects

E. Supporting verbal points with text—computer and overhead presentations, posters and flipcharts, whiteboards and chalkboards

F. Supporting with sound—audio recordings

SITUATIONS

_____ 1. You are part of a panel of four people in your music history class who must give a 45-minute presentation on the life and works of Beethoven.

Delivery method: _____

_____ 2. You are a dean in the college's admissions or institutional research office. You have ten minutes to present data on the changing demographics of your student population in the past two years.

Delivery method: _____

_____ 3. You are taking an American literature class, and each student must do a five-minute background presentation before the class discussion of literature. You are required to prepare a one-page handout with relevant information for the class. You chose the topic "Conventions of Gothic Literature," which is to precede the study of Edgar Allan Poe. What will you include on your handout?

Delivery method: _____

_____ 4. You work for a large home-improvement chain. You will be presenting a one-hour workshop on installing a molded shower enclosure for customers with limited skills.

Delivery method: _____

_____ 5. You are studying dental hygiene. You need to give patients a five-minute lesson on correct flossing after the checkup and cleaning is done.

Delivery method:_____

_____ 6. You are the president of a prominent community organization, and you have fifteen minutes to present the accomplishments and background of a recipient of a lifetime community service award.

Delivery method: _____

Chapter 32	**Making Oral Presentations**

Exercise B	**32d Preparing Visual Aids—Using Presentation Software**

Using presentation software, such as Powerpoint, and the information below, create a presentation.

1. Target Audience: Prospective students and their families for Millard Fillmore University.

2. Facts: Information provided in Exercise A: 9a entitled Understanding Inductive Reasoning of this workbook.

3. Graphics: Use one or more of the Excel graphs from Exercise A11b Evaluating Visuals in this workbook or create your own graphics.

Use the following checklist to evaluate your presentation in partners, small groups, or whole-class discussion.

LAYOUT

1. Have you selected an appealing but professional background template?

2. Briefly discuss the benefits and drawbacks of a dark background with light lettering versus a light background with dark lettering. Are you going to project this presentation in a particular room environment? Are you going to provide slide handouts?

ORGANIZATION

1. Does the first slide include the title of the presentation, the presenters, and the date of presentation?

2. Does the second slide provide an overview of the presentation? Do the topics match the headings of the content slides?

3. Do all content slides follow a parallel structure?

4. Have graphics been planned to accompany text?

5. Does the final slide provide contact or follow-up information?

CONTENT

1. Does each content slide have a title that matches the overview slide?

2. Is information provided in small increments with bulleted or numbered points? Is the hierarchy of points clear and logical?

3. Have you avoided crowding, overly detailed graphics, and overly small print? Check the presentation by projecting and viewing from various points in the room where it will be viewed.

4. Is each slide accurate? Check for errors in spelling, punctuation, and word usage. Above all, check for faulty parallelism between points.

Chapter 33	**Building Simple Sentences**

Exercise A	**33a Constructing Simple Sentences**

In each of the following sentences, underline the subject once and the predicate twice. Then label direct objects (do), indirect objects (io), subject complements (sc), and object complements (oc).

EXAMPLE: <u>Few people</u> <u><u>have defined American popular culture</u></u> the way Walt
Disney did.

do

1. Walter Elias Disney was born on December 5, 1901, in Chicago, Illinois.

2. He was the fourth son in the family.

3. Walt's father, Elias, moved his family several times over the years in pursuit of work.

4. Walt joined the Red Cross Ambulance Corps in 1918 by lying about his age.

5. The Kansas City Slide Company offered Walt a job making animated commercials after World War I.

6. Walt studied animation and began to make his own cartoons.

7. He started a company called Laugh-O-Gram Films in 1921.

8. Unfortunately, Walt had many financial setbacks as he tried to sell his animated films.

9. He declared bankruptcy in Kansas City and purchased a train ticket to California.

10. He carried the unfinished film that he called "Alice's Wonderland" with him.

Chapter 33 Building Simple Sentences

Exercise B   33b Identifying Phrases and Clauses

The following groups of words come from the preceding exercise. Label each word group IC for independent clause, DC for dependent clause, or P for phrase.

EXAMPLE: __P__ In Chicago, Illinois.

_____ 1. On December 5, 1901.

_____ 2. He was the fourth son in the family.

_____ 3. Walt's father, Elias, moved his family several times.

_____ 4. By lying about his age.

_____ 5. Making animated commercials after the war.

_____ 6. Walt studied animation.

_____ 7. He started a company.

_____ 8. As he tried to sell his animated films.

_____ 9. He purchased a train ticket to California.

_____10. That he called "Alice's Wonderland."

Chapter 33 | Building Simple Sentences

Exercise C	33c Expanding Simple Sentences—Adjectives, Adverbs, and Prepositional Phrases

Label all the descriptive adjectives (adj) and adverbs (adv) in the following sentences. Place square brackets around prepositional phrases.

                                      adj.   adv.

EXAMPLE: [From every point] [in the Magic Kingdom] [in Orlando,] guests

                            adj.

      can see the beautiful Cinderella's Castle.

1. As guests walk through the castle, they will see ornate and detailed murals from the fairy tale.

2. Cinderella's two wicked stepsisters have vividly colored faces.

3. In the fairy tale, one sister is described as "green with envy" while the other is "red with rage."

4. The muralist has captured the expressions of the malicious sisters perfectly.

5. Cinderella and her handsome Prince Charming will ride the magical coach and live "happily ever after."

Chapter 33	Building Simple Sentences

Exercise D	33c Expanding Simple Sentences—Verbal Phrases

Combine each sentence pair below to create one simple sentence that contains a participial phrase, a gerund phrase, or an infinitive phrase.

After entering , *you*
EXAMPLE: ~~Enter~~ the Magic Kingdom at Main Street U.S.A. ~~You~~ turn to
the left to visit Adventure Land.

1. The Jungle Cruise features all the great rivers of the world. The great rivers include the Amazon, the Nile, and the Congo.

2. Beyond the Jungle Cruise is the popular Pirates of the Caribbean with animated pirates. The pirates pillage the Spanish Main.

3. No trip is complete without a visit to the Haunted Mansion. The Haunted Mansion features hundreds of holographic ghosts at every turn.

4. The ghosts want to leave with the guests. The ghosts board each guest's car.

5. Guests see themselves in a mirror. They are accompanied by a "hitchhiker."

| Chapter 34 | **Building Compound and Complex Sentences** |

Exercise A   34a Building Compound Sentences

Add appropriate coordinating conjunctions, conjunctive adverbs, or correlative conjunctions to combine each pair of sentences into one well-constructed compound sentence that retains the meaning of the original pair. Be sure to use correct punctuation.

EXAMPLE: On December 12th, the Feast of Our Lady of Guadalupe is cele-
, and
brated Pope John Paul II declared the date a Liturgical Holy Day
^
for the whole continent in 1999.

1. In 1521, the capital city of the Aztec empire fell to the Spanish *conquistadors*. Within a few years, several million inhabitants converted to Christianity.

2. A native of the region of Tlayacac was named Cuauhtlatoatzin. Today he is known to the world as Juan Diego.

3. Around 1524 or 1525 Cuauhtlatoatzin was converted and baptized as a Roman Catholic. He received his Christian name of Juan Diego at that time.

4. In 1531, Juan Diego had his miraculous vision of a Lady from Heaven at Tepeyac. The Lady instructed Juan Diego to have the bishop build a temple on the site.

5. The Lady left an image of herself on Juan Diego's *tilma*. This familiar image is known as Our Lady of Guadalupe.

6. Juan Diego wore the *tilma*, a simple cloth mantle made of the rough fibers of the maguey cactus. Juan Diego went barefoot.

7. The image on the *tilma* should have deteriorated in twenty years. It remains in good shape to this day.

8. An Indian named Antonio Valeriano wrote a document in the native Nahuatl language. This document tells story of the apparitions.

9. The document is known as the Valeriano Relation. The document is also known as the Nican Mopohua.

10. The bishop, Juan de Zumarraga, did not believe Juan Diego's story of his vision. He asked for proof.

Chapter 34 | Building Compound and Complex Sentences

Exercise B | 34b Building Complex Sentences

Use a subordinate conjunction or relative pronoun to combine each of the following pairs of sentences into one well-constructed complex sentence.

        After   *vision,*

EXAMPLE: Bishop Zumarraga doubted Juan Diego's story of the ~~vision~~ Juan Diego prayed to the Lady for some further proof.

1. Juan Diego continued his visits to the Lady. She then provided him with a miracle for the bishop.

2. The weather was too cold for flowers to bloom. The Lady showed Juan Diego hundreds of roses in bloom to bring to the bishop.

3. Juan Diego died in 1548. The archbishop of Mexico approved the visions and built a church.

4. Copies of the image of Our Lady of Guadalupe went abroad from Mexico. One copy went to King Philip II of Spain.

5. The Virgin of Guadalupe was declared Patroness of Latin America in 1910. She was declared Patroness of the Americas in 1946.

6. Pope John Paul II began the canonization process for declaring Juan Diego a saint. The process was completed in July 2002.

Chapter 35   Writing Varied Sentences

Exercise A   35b Combining Choppy Simple Sentences

Using coordination, subordination, and embedding, revise this string of choppy simple sentences into a more varied and interesting set of paragraphs.

Richard Henry Pratt was an officer in the 10th Cavalry. He served after the American Civil War. He commanded African-American Buffalo Soldiers. He commanded Indian Scouts. He came in contact with Kiowa, Cheyenne, and Arapaho Indians on reservations. He saw that the food supplies to the reservations were inadequate. He understood why the warriors continued to raid the settlers. He was disgusted with the Bureau of Indian Affairs.

Hostile Indian warriors were imprisoned by the U.S. government in St. Augustine, Florida. Pratt was in charge. Pratt decided to train these warriors. He dressed them in military uniforms. He cut their hair. He drilled and trained them. He had volunteers teach them to read.

Pratt and various Indian Reformers did not believe in extermination policies. They decided on a plan of assimilation instead. Pratt saw a model in the Hampton Institute of Virginia. The Hampton Institute was a boarding school. It was created to educate African-American children.

Pratt obtained permission from the federal government. He was given access to the Carlisle Barracks. The Carlisle Barracks was in Pennsylvania. It was an old cavalry post.

Pratt traveled west. He spoke to leaders of the Rosebud reservation. He spoke to leaders of the Pine Ridge Agency. He recruited Native American children for his new school. One of the students was Luther Standing Bear. Luther Standing Bear wrote of his experiences.

Chapter 35 | Writing Varied Sentences

Exercise B | 35e Varying Sentence Openings

The following is a short passage from Luther Standing Bear's *My People, the Sioux* (University of Nebraska Press, 1975). Label the various types of sentence opening he uses.

One day we had a strange experience. We were all called together by the interpreter and told that we were to have our hair cut off. We listened to what he had to say, but we did not reply. This was something that would require some thought, so that evening the big boys held a council, and I recall very distinctly that Nakpa Kesela, or Robert American Horse, made a serious speech. Said he, "If I am to learn the ways of the white people, I can do it just as well with my hair on." To this we all exclaimed "Hau!"—meaning that we agreed with him.

In spite of this meeting, a few days later we saw some white men come inside the school grounds carrying big chairs. The interpreter told us these were the men who had come to cut out hair. We did not watch to see where the chairs were carried, as it was school time, and we went to our classroom. One of the big boys named Ya Slo, or Whistler, was missing. In a short time he came in with his hair cut off. They then called another boy out, and when he returned, he also wore short hair. In this way we were called out one by one.

When I saw most of them with short hair, I began to feel anxious to be "in style" and wanted mine cut, too. Finally I was called out of the schoolroom, and when I went into the next room, the barber was waiting for me. He motioned for me to sit down, and then he commenced work. But when my hair was cut short, it hurt my feelings to such an extent that the tears came into my eyes. I do not recall whether the barber noticed my agitation or not, nor did I care. All I was thinking about was that hair he had taken away from me.

Chapter 35 · Writing Varied Sentences

Exercise C · **35f Varying Standard Word Order**

The following sentences use conventional word order. Revise each in one of two ways: Either invert the sentence or vary the word order by placing words between the subject and the verb.

1. Pratt was committed to his belief in assimilation and continued to train Indians to imitate the white man.

   _____

   _____

2. Many children died who succumbed to diseases such as tuberculosis and smallpox.

   _____

   _____

3. A cemetery was established for the children who died from diseases and hardships.

   _____

   _____

4. Apache children lived under horrifying conditions when Geronimo and his people were exiled to Florida.

   _____

   _____

5. More graves represent Apache children who were sent to Carlisle from Florida.

   _____

   _____

Chapter 36 Writing Emphatic Sentences

Exercise A   36a Conveying Emphasis through Word Order

Revise the following sentences to make them more emphatic by relocating words, phrases, or clauses to shift focus.

EXAMPLE: The Harlem Renaissance refers to a movement between World War I and the mid-1930s when cultural accomplishments of African Americans blossomed.

REVISED: Cultural accomplishments of African Americans blossomed during the Harlem Renaissance, a movement between World War I and the mid-1930s.

1. One of the people who inspired the movement was W. E. B. DuBois, who organized the first Pan African Congress in 1919.

   _____

   _____

   _____

   _____

   _____

2. W. E. B. DuBois had also written an influential book entitled *The Souls of Black Folks* and had helped to found the National Association for the Advancement of Colored People.

   _____

   _____

   _____

   _____

   _____

3. African Americans began to have a place in the performing arts with a musical review entitled *Shuffle Along* written by Eubie Blake and Noble Sissle and performed by African-American actors.

_____

_____

_____

_____

_____

4. Literature flourished as African-American writers, such as Claude McKay, Jean Toomer, Langston Hughes, and Zora Neal Hurston, published works.

_____

_____

_____

_____

_____

5. Marcus Garvey was defining important religious values when he founded the African Orthodox Church in 1921.

_____

_____

_____

_____

_____

Chapter 36 | Writing Emphatic Sentences

Exercise B | 36b Conveying Emphasis through Sentence Structure

Revise the following sentences for emphasis. Achieve greater emphasis with the following strategies:

- Change passive verbs to active.
- Use parallelism and balanced sentences.
- Use cumulative and periodic sentences.

EXAMPLE: ~~More versatile, experimental writers were~~ Langston Hughes and
were versatile, experimental writers;
Zora Neal Hurston~~, while~~ Countee Cullen and Jean Toomer were
^
more traditional and literary.

1. Hughes was raised mainly by his maternal grandmother because his parents were separated and his father went to Mexico.

2. He attended Columbia University but a degree was not earned because he left to travel.

3. Hughes kept writing poetry and his first volume of poems was published in 1926 when he was twenty-four.

4. Hughes wanted to create an authentic voice for African Americans by using the rhythms of music and everyday speech in his poetry.

5. Hughes was challenged by the risk of creating stereotypes of African Americans for his largely white reading audience.

Chapter 37 | Writing Concise Sentences

Exercise A   37a Eliminating Wordiness

Edit the following sentences to remove deadwood, utility words, and circumlocution.

> EXAMPLE: ~~At the present time,~~ ^{*Today*} we can visit a ~~little~~ bit of prehistory ~~in the~~ ^{*near*} ^ ~~vicinity of~~ Los Angeles. ^

1. In the Page Museum, it exhibits hundreds of fossil bones found in the La Brea Tar Pits.

2. It is important to note that more than one million bones representing more than 230 species of vertebrates have been recovered.

3. The fossils are a dark brown in color because they are colored by a saturation of asphalt in the bones.

4. Skeletons are assembled with steel and wire for the purpose of showing the structures of prehistoric animals.

5. Due to the fact that some skeletal parts were cartilage, resin or plaster is used for reconstructions.

Chapter 37 | Writing Concise Sentences

Exercise B | 37b and c Eliminating Unnecessary Repetition and Tightening Rambling Sentences

Edit the following paragraph to create concise sentences. Remove unnecessary repetition and eliminate nonessential wording.

During the last Ice Age, many animals that lived then and are now extinct roamed the region now known as Rancho La Brea. The time period for this Ice Age was between 40,000 to 10,000 years ago. There were a number of species trapped in the tar pits including saber-toothed cats and mammoths. Additional species include various birds and wolves. Animals would come in contact with the sticky asphalt pools and would become trapped and would die. Even the remains of one human being, which was a woman with a bad sinus infection that may have made her delirious, have been found in the tar pits. Even to this very day, small animals and invertebrates are occasionally trapped in the warm, oozing asphalt.

_____

_____

_____

_____

_____

_____

_____

_____

| Chapter 38 | Revising Sentence Fragments |

| Exercise A | 38a–c Revising Sentence Fragments |

Revise the following paragraphs to eliminate all sentence fragments. Some fragments require a subject or a complete verb; others represent a variety of dependent clauses and phrases.

A traditional form of Japanese theatre is Kabuki. Which dates to the seventeenth century. All the actors are men. Highly trained in a stylized form of acting. Some actors specialize in female impersonation. The Kabuki characters are recognized stereotypes. Such as the warrior or *samurai* and the courtesan. The audience recognizes specific ways of walking, gesture, and dress to identify characters.

Elements of Kabuki theatre include vivid and complex costumes and makeup. As well as instrumental music and dance. Colors are used symbolically, and makeup is elaborate. Female impersonators wear beautiful wigs. Faces and hands painted white. Drums and string instruments play in the background. To create a pace and rhythm for the action.

Kabuki plots are often tragic and violent. One type of Kabuki story involves transformation. Shape-shifting from an animal such as a spider to a human form may occur. To create terror. Love stories often end in double suicides. Because of forbidden love. Blood will pour from wounds in the form of long red silk scarfs. Death is enacted vividly, and expressions of anguish are frozen to enhance emotion.

Chapter 38 Revising Sentence Fragments

Exercise B   38a–c Revising Sentence Fragments

Revise the following paragraphs to eliminate all sentence fragments. Some fragments require a subject or a complete verb; others represent a variety of dependent clauses and phrases.

Chad Hurley and Steve Chen are probably not household names, but they have transformed the ways we create and view video. And made $1.65 billion almost overnight. Hurley and Chen are the founders of YouTube. Which they sold to Google in 2006.

Hurley majored in computer science at Indiana University of Pennsylvania and began working at PayPal in 1999. A new company. There he met Steve Chen, an engineer. Chen was born in Taipei. Attended the prestigious Illinois Math and Science Academy and the University of Illinois at Urbana-Champaign. Jawed Karim, another engineer at Paypal. Together, they conceived the idea for YouTube. But they do not agree on the exact details of its creation.

People may post and view videos of their choice on YouTube. The site popularizes "Featured Videos." Links to MySpace. Pornography is flagged by users and removed by YouTube. Investors wished to purchase the site. Because of potential for advertising and reaching so many consumers. Hurley and Chen still manage the site. Even though Google now owns it.

Chapter 39 | Revising Comma Splices and Fused Sentences

Exercise A | **39b–e Revising with Periods, Semicolons, Coordinating Conjunctions, Subordinating Conjunctions, and Relative Pronouns**

Revise the following paragraphs to correct all comma splices and fused sentences. Make suitable choices of periods, semicolons, coordinating conjunctions, subordinating conjunctions, and relative pronouns to create paragraph coherence and logical relationships.

One of the most beautiful historic homes in America is Monticello, the home of Thomas Jefferson, it is built in Roman neoclassical style. Jefferson designed the home, construction began in 1769. Further remodeling began in 1796 the home was complete in 1809. The home is filled with Jefferson's innovations and is open to the public for tours.

Jefferson used both mirrors and skylights to provide greater illumination in the rooms of his home. Mirrors on opposite walls create an illusion of greater size, skylights provide natural lighting to a number of rooms. Tall windows that opened both from the top and the bottom provided better ventilation as well as lighting.

Jefferson invented the dumbwaiter so that food could be brought to the dining room without servants cluttering the room. Cooking took place in a separate cabin. Most plantation homes had separate cooking cabins, risk of fire was too great to allow cooking within the plantation home. Food was rushed to the lower level of the house it was then hoisted on the dumbwaiter.

Jefferson died in debt, Jefferson's children were forced to sell the plantation. Monticello was bequeathed to the government by Uriah P. Levy, who purchased the home in 1834. During the Civil War, the house was seized by the Confederacy, the home's ownership was then contested. In 1923, the Thomas Jefferson Foundation purchased the home and owns it to this day.

Chapter 39 Revising Run-ons

Exercise B **39b–e Revising with Periods, Semicolons, Coordinating Conjunctions, Subordinating Conjunctions, and Relative Pronouns**

Revise the following paragraphs to correct all comma splices and fused sentences. Make suitable choices of periods, semicolons, coordinating conjunctions, subordinating conjunctions, and relative pronouns to create paragraph coherence and logical relationships.

Craig Kielburger, an amazing young Canadian, founded "Free the Children," the largest international network of children helping children, when he was only twelve years old. He travels the world speaking in defense of children's rights he has authored several books, and has appeared in a number of television programs and magazine articles.

Craig and his brother Marc wrote *Me to We: Turning Self-Help on Its Head* it is part of their Take Action! series. The book provides inspiration stories of the Kielburgers' global experiences in helping children around the world. After each chapter, a famous philanthropist provides a personal story of transformation, these writers include Oprah Winfrey, Richard Gere, Archbishop Desmond Tutu, and Dr. Jane Goodall, among others.

I was fortunate enough to hear Craig speak at a conference in Arizona. He had just flown in from Sweden because his organization has been nominated for the third time for the Nobel Peace Prize. Craig is a tirelessly energetic young man committed to human rights and education, he inspires others to take action he is living proof that young people can take action and make a difference in the lives of others.

Chapter 40 | Revising Misplaced and Dangling Modifiers

Exercise A | 40a and c Revising Misplaced and Dangling Modifiers

Revise the following sentences to correct a misplaced or a dangling modifier.

EXAMPLE: ~~With her blue hair piled high,~~ Homer Simpson sees his wife
Marge as the beauty of her family.
, with her blue hair piled high,
^

1. Husky-voiced denizens of the Department of Motor Vehicles, Marge easily outshines her protective older sisters, Patty and Selma Bouvier.

2. Patty and Selma devote their lives to chain-smoking, harassing Homer, and watching *MacGyver*, who is not good enough for Marge.

3. Falling in love with Sideshow Bob, the sisters were in danger of being separated if one were to marry.

4. Bart rescued his aunt Patty from death on her honeymoon realizing that Sideshow Bob was planning to murder her.

5. Both Patty and Selma made Homer their slave, loaning him money when he couldn't pay the mortgage and wanting to keep Marge from knowing.

Chapter 40 | Revising Misplaced and Dangling Modifiers

Exercise B | 40a and c Revising Misplaced and Dangling Modifiers

Revise the following sentences to correct a misplaced or dangling modifier.

EXAMPLE: trackers in the Democratic Republic of Congo seek the great ape known as the bonobo, <u>a creature slaughtered for food and possibly endangered</u>.

1. The bonobo is our closest primate relative along with the chimpanzee.

2. Scientists realized that bonobos in 1929 were a distinct species and not just a smaller chimpanzee.

3. Unlike chimpanzees, though they have an aggressive side, bonobos are gentler and more playful.

4. Though conservationists have placed a ban on eating bonobo meat, knowing the animals are endangered, some tribal villagers believe the meat will make them powerful.

5. Provided with funding to prevent poaching, the bonobos are less likely to be killed by villagers.

Chapter 41 Using Parallelism

Exercise A   41a Using Parallelism Effectively

Combine each sentence group into one sentence that uses parallel structure.

EXAMPLE: When Edgar Allen Poe wrote "The Raven," he needed a talking
bird. He considered a parrot. He also considered a raven.
     : he   or

1. Poe explained his purpose in writing "The Raven" in "The Philosophy of Composition." He also explained his method and his stylistic choices.

2. Poe believed a poem should be read in one sitting for the full effect. It should not be too long. It should not be too short.

3. Poe wanted to use a refrain. He wanted the refrain to gain further meaning as the poem progressed. He wanted the refrain to fit his metrical pattern, too.

4. Poe decided he would use a talking bird to utter the refrain. He would use the bird to address the poem's speaker.

5. The poem's speaker is a grieving man who has lost his love named Lenore. The speaker is also sleepless.

6. A winter storm rages outside the speaker's study. A tapping is heard at the window.

7. Poe chose the raven because it is capable of speaking. He also chose the raven because it is large and black.

8. The raven enters the study. It perches on the white marble bust of Pallas. It speaks its only word, "Nevermore."

9. "Nevermore" becomes the answer to all the speaker's questions. The answer first creates humor. Later it creates despair.

10. Poe found one word to meet all of his needs. He wanted a refrain. He wanted the meaning to change. He found a word to rhyme with "Lenore."

Chapter 41 | Using Parallelism

Exercise B | 41b Revising Faulty Parallelism

Correct the faulty parallelism in the following sentences.

EXAMPLE: The raven is noted for its large size, its lustrous black feathers,
        its
    and ~~it has a~~ raucous cry.
        ^

1. The raven appears in the folklore of Native Americans, and a
   legend exists about ravens and the English monarchy.

2. A visitor to the Tower of London will learn that a flock of ravens
   must remain on the property or the lack of ravens will cause the
   fall of the monarchy.

3. The speaker of Poe's "The Raven" refers to the royal appearance
   and association with the past, but no connection is made to
   North American legends.

4. The raven appears in the artwork of Native American tribes
   from the Pacific Northwest; artwork from the Southwest, Plains,
   and tribes of the East does not include the raven.

5. Poe was relying on a European tradition in Gothic literature to
   create his dark imagery that is terrifying.

Chapter 42	Revising Awkward and Confusing Sentences

Exercise A   42a Revising Unwarranted Shifts

The following sentences have unwarranted shifts in verb tense, person, or number, or between active and passive voice. Eliminate the shifts.

EXAMPLE: One of the bravest women in literature is Scheherezade, the brilliant queen and storyteller who ~~narrated~~ *narrates* The Thousand and One Nights, a collection of stories from Arabic, Persian, and Indian traditions.

1. Scheherezade is compelled to tell captivating stories to her husband, King Shahryar, to save her life because his previous wives were killed by him to prevent infidelity.

2. The reader is as captivated as her husband because we are absorbed in the suspense and excitement of her tales.

3. Each night, Scheherezade wove a tale of magic, intrigue, love, and treachery; at dawn, she provides a "cliffhanger" ending to keep her listeners returning for more.

4. Scheherezade shows gullible characters who are deceived by their evil spouse, but she also punishes the wicked with violent deaths.

5. Violence is portrayed in many of Scheherezade's stories, but, more important, she shows the power of language to persuade and move hearts to goodness.

6. Good characters who call out to Allah in their time of need had their prayers answered, while you see wicked characters consistently punished.

7. After many nights of storytelling, King Shahryar has learned to love and trust his wife, he no longer wants to kill her, and three children are fathered by him.

Chapter 42	Revising Awkward and Confusing Sentences

Exercise B   42b Revising Mixed Constructions

Revise the following sentences to eliminate mixed constructions.

                                                          , the Fisherman
EXAMPLE: By casting his net four times in the ocean trapped a mysterious
                                                            ^
copper jar.

1. Even though he did not catch a fish did not mean that the Fisherman had a bad day.

2. He rubbed the copper jar was what made the Genie pop out.

3. By roaring a threat to kill the Fisherman made the Fisherman question his good deed in freeing the Genie.

4. The Genie told his story of centuries of captivity was what made him so angry.

5. Though the Fisherman tricked the Genie back into the jar by using his brain caused the Genie to comply with the wishes of the Fisherman.

Chapter 42   Revising Awkward and Confusing Sentences

Exercise C   42c Revising Faulty Predication

Revise the following sentences to eliminate faulty predication.

EXAMPLE: One of the best tales from *The Thousand and One Nights* ~~was~~ *tells of the time*

~~when~~ King Yunan was deceived by his evil Vizier.

1. The reason King Yunan was in trouble was because he suffered from incurable leprosy.

2. The arrival of the wise Sage Duban was when the conflict began with the jealous Vizier.

3. Sage Duban cured King Yunan completely, but the reason the Vizier became jealous was because the King rewarded the Sage so well.

4. The reason King Yunan was confused was because he believed his Vizier saw evil in the Sage.

5. The undoing of King Yunan was when he executed the Sage and died as a consequence of his gullibility.

Chapter 43 | Choosing Words

Exercise A | 43a Choosing an Appropriate Level of Diction

The following passages are taken from the works identified in parentheses. Label each passage as formal (F) or informal (I). Underline key words that indicate informal diction.

_____ 1. "The polie is men in black who gets kids and send them to Tijuana, says Popi. Whenever you see them, run, because they hate you, says Popi. She grabs Macky by his sleeve and they crawl under a table of bargain cassettes. Macky's nose is running, and when he sniffles, she puts her finger to her lips. She peeks from behind the poster of Vincente Fernandez to see Raoul's father putting keys and stuff from his pockets onto the hood of the polie car." (Helena Maria Viramontes, "The Cariboo Café")

_____ 2. "The Center for Urban Problems (CUP), as Washington's largest organization dealing with police-community relations, invites your investment in a $66,240 special project to improve community relations with minorities. We are encouraged that the Law Enforcement Foundation supports innovative projects that improve the delivery of police services." (Mike Markel, *Technical Communication*)

_____ 3. "My one talent was I could always make money. I had a touch for it, unusual in a Chippewa. From the first I was different that way, and everyone recognized it. I was the only kid they let in the American Legion Hall to shine shoes, for example, and one Christmas I sold spiritual bouquets for the mission door to door." (Speaker: Lyman Lamartine. Louise Erdrich, *Love Medicine*)

_____ 4. "Sister Mary Martin de Porres played the clarinet and sometimes, when she was troubled or sleep was elusive, wrote her own music. Tonight she woke, starting, from an odd dream. For a long moment, she vaguely believed she was at home in Lincoln." (Louise Erdrich, *Love Medicine*)

_____ 5. "[Darcy] McNickle's first novel, The Surrounded, was published in 1936, two years after the Indian Reorganization Act was passed near the end of the Depression in the United States. This new policy ended the federal allotment of communal land to individuals and provided for the establishment of representative governments on reservation." (Gerald Vizenor, *Native American Literature*)

Sources

Viramontes, Helena Maria. "The Cariboo Café." *Hispanic American Literature.* Ed. Nicolas Kanellos. Berkeley: HarperCollins Literary Mosaic Series, 1995. 170.

Markel, Mike. *Technical Communication.* 7th ed. Boston: Bedford/St. Martin's, 2004. 457.
Erdrich, Louise. *Love Medicine.* New York: Perennial/HarperCollins, 1993. 181.

Vizenor, Gerald. *Native American Literature.* Ed. Gerald Vizenor. Berkeley: HarperCollins Literary Mosaic Series, 1995. 4.

Chapter 43 Choosing Words

Exercise B   **43b Choosing the Right Word**

The following passage uses vague language. Replace the underlined words with more precise choices.

Louise wrote <u>an interesting book</u> called *Love Medicine* in 1984 and expanded it in 1993. Various Native American characters from three generations <u>tell about</u> their experiences. They <u>talk about things</u> like conflicts over land, religion, and <u>other aspects of life</u>. Two brothers, Nector and Eli Kashpaw, were each raised to learn about <u>opposite things</u>. Nector was sent to boarding school to learn the white man's skills, and Eli stayed home to learn native ways. Nector loves Lulu Nanapush but <u>gets</u> Marie Lazarre for his wife instead. Lulu has eight sons by different fathers, so the tribe <u>does not think she is very nice</u>.

Chapter 43 — Choosing Words

Exercise C   43c Using Figures of Speech

One of the narrators of Louise Erdrich's *Love Medicine,* Lulu Nanapush, writes with lavish figurative language. Identify the underlined figures of speech as metaphor (m), simile (s), personification (p), hyperbole (h), or under-statement (u).

"I never grew from the curve of my mother's arms. I still wanted to anchor myself against her. But she had tore [*sic*] herself away from the run of my life like a riverbank. She had vanished, a great surrounding shore, leaving me to spill out alone. "I wanted to fill her tracks, but luck ran out the holes. My wishes were worn soles. I stumbled in those shoes of desire. Following my mother, I ran away from the government school."

Source: Erdrich, Louise. *Love Medicine.* New York: Perennial/HarperCollins, 1993. 68.

Chapter 44 | Using a Dictionary

Visit the Web site for the *Oxford English Dictionary* and access the word *telemedicine*. Answer the following questions about the word.

1. Which part of speech is the word *telemedicine*?

   _____

2. In what year did the word *telemedicine* appear in a publication?

   _____

3. Where did it appear?

   _____

4. What does "Nexis" mean in the entry for 1987?

   _____

   _____

5. Is an etymology given for the word? What does the prefix *tele-* usually mean? Where could you find this information?

   _____

   _____

   _____

   _____

Chapter 45	**Improving Spelling**

Exercise A	**45a Understanding Spelling and Pronunciation—Homophones**

One problem for students is the usage of homophones, words that are pronounced alike but spelled differently. They are actually usage errors, and a spell checker will not recognize a misuse as a spelling error. Underline the correct homophone in the sentences below.

1. Some of the most chilling and dramatic (effects, affects) appear in the black-and-white movies of Alfred Hitchcock.

2. No one can be (bored, board) or apathetic during the shrill screech of violins, which accompanies the famous stabbing in the shower in *Psycho*.

3. (Its, It's) well known that the (allusion, illusion) of blood in that movie was created with chocolate syrup.

4. Hitchcock had to (device, devise) a way to make birds attack his actors in *The Birds*.

5. A small number of birds were trained to attack the heads of actors as they stood still, so the birds pursued the actors as they ran and attacked the (sight, site, cite) when the actors stopped moving.

6. Without portraying explicit violence, Hitchcock made his audiences (conscience, conscious) of the presence of sinister forces.

7. For all the benefits of computerized special (affects, effects), few movies today can compete with these cinematic masterpieces for (there, their) sheer horror.

Chapter 45	Improving Spelling

Exercise B	45a–c Various Spelling Issues

The following paragraphs represent a variety of common spelling errors. Underline the correct spelling of the words in parentheses.

Since 1901, the Nobel Prize has been granted to (candidates, canidates) in five areas: physics, chemistry, medicine, literature, and peace. These prizes are awarded to those who have "conferred the greatest benefit on mankind." These distinguished recipients are characterized by (brilliance, brillience) and (excellance, excellence). In 1968, the Bank of Sweden added a sixth prize for Economic Sciences in honor of Alfred Nobel, the founder of the prizes. Recipients must be alive at the time of nomination, but a (deceased, diseased) person can receive the prize if he or she (dies, dyes) between the naming in October and the Prize Award Ceremony on December 10. The award ceremony is held (annually, anually) in Stockholm, the (capitol, capital) of Sweden.

The first Nobel Prize for Literature went to poet Sully Prudhomme, whose pen name is René François Armand, in 1901. Several Americans have received and (excepted, accepted) the award, including the novelist Sinclair Lewis in 1930, the (playwright, playright) Eugene O'Neill in 1936, the novelist and biographer Pearl Buck in 1938, and the novelist William Faulkner in 1949. In 1954, Ernest Hemingway (received, recieved) the award for his mastery of the art of narrative. John Steinbeck was (cited, sited) for his realism and sympathetic (humour, humor) in 1962. In 1976, Saul Bellow (won, one) the award for his subtle (analysis, analyses) of contemporary culture. The (criteria, criterias) for Toni Morrison's award in 1993 included her visionary force and (brilliant, brillient) portrayals of American (reality, realty).

Name _____ Date _____ Score _____

Parts of Speech

Exercise A   46a–h All Parts of Speech

Review all parts of speech in Chapter 46 of your handbook. Identify the part of speech for every word in the following passage. Use the abbreviation in parentheses for each part: noun (n), pronoun (pron), verb (v), adjective (adj), adverb (adv), preposition (prep), conjunction (conj), and interjection (i).

Before September 11, 2001, few people were aware of the problems in Afghanistan or knew the history of the ancient city of Kabul. Kabul has a fascinating history linked to the Ten Lost Tribes of Israel. Several Afghani tribes consider themselves to be descendents of King Saul of the Old Testament. The exiled Royal Family of Afghanistan considers itself descended from the tribe of Benjamin.

The legend of the city of Kabul is intriguing, too. This legend states that Cain, Adam's first son who killed his brother Abel, is buried in Kabul. The name *Kabul* is a blend of "Cain" and "Abel." Cain was ancient when he arrived in Kabul. He had been driven from city to city. No one would welcome him except the kind people of Kabul. They gave him shelter. He was eventually buried there. Cain was a tragic figure, and the tragedy continues in this ancient place.

Chapter 46 — Parts of Speech

Exercise B   46a–h All Parts of Speech

Look again at the parts of speech in the preceding Exercise A and the information on parts of speech in your handbook. Write down an example of the following types of parts of speech.

NOUNS

A proper noun _____

A common noun _____

PRONOUNS

A personal pronoun _____

A relative pronoun _____

A reflexive pronoun _____

VERBS

A main verb _____

A linking verb _____

An auxiliary (helping) verb _____

A verbal _____

ADJECTIVES

A descriptive adjective _____

An article _____

A demonstrative pronoun used as an adjective _____

ADVERBS

An adverb answering "when" _____

PREPOSITIONS

Any preposition _____

CONJUNCTIONS

A subordinating conjunction _____

A coordinating conjunction _____

Chapter 47	**Using Nouns and Pronouns**

Exercise A **47a–b Understanding and Determining Pronoun Case in Special Situations**

Underline the correct case for the pronouns in the parentheses.

1. On September 25, 2003, Edward Said, (who, whom) was a noted scholar and literary critic at Columbia University, died of leukemia.

2. Many knew (he, him) as the author of *Orientalism* and an advocate for the cause of Palestinian independence.

3. Few also knew that (he, him) and Daniel Barenboim, Jewish conductor of the Chicago Symphony Orchestra, had a long-standing relationship.

4. (He, him) and Said co-founded the West-Eastern Divan in 1999, an opportunity for Israeli and Arab musicians to work toward the goal of (them, their) achieving understanding between the two groups.

5. In 2002, Spain awarded the Prince of Asturias Concord Prize to Barenboim and (he, him) for their efforts in bringing peace to the Middle East.

6. Said defended the rights of the Islamic Palestinians, but his wife and (he, him) were Christians, (he, him) an Episcopalian and (she, her) a Quaker.

7. Said criticized Yasser Arafat, (who, whom) signed the Oslo Peace Accord in 1993, for making a bad arrangement for the Palestinians.

8. Said sought peace, but (he, him) and other defenders of Palestine are also seeking justice and independence from Israel.

Chapter 47 — Using Nouns and Pronouns

Exercise B   47c Revising Pronoun Reference Errors

The following paragraphs have pronouns with ambiguous, remote, or non-existent antecedents. Locate the pronouns and revise the sentences to correct the reference problems.

Two very different men who contributed to the advancement of African Americans after the Emancipation Proclamation were Booker T. Washington and W. E. B. DuBois. Both wanted educational opportunities and political rights for their race, but their approaches were at odds. Washington was born into slavery, and this may have contributed to his more cautious approach to achieving rights. In Washington's book, *Up From Slavery*, he tells of his early days on a Virginia plantation and of the arrival of the news of freedom. It was a badly maintained place because the slaves took no pride in their work and were not trained adequately. However, some slaves were reluctant to leave their masters, and they made compromising arrangements. Eventually, Washington worked hard, learned to read and write, and became an activist.

In 1895, Washington spoke to a crowd of more than two thousand people at the Atlanta Exposition. Critics of his position, including DuBois, saw Washington as too compromising. He sought educational and employment opportunities in the trades. He praised the South and white Southerners.

In contrast, W. E. B. DuBois was born in Massachusetts, a free man. Unlike Washington, he did not experience slavery or dire poverty. He was well educated at Fisk, Harvard, and the University of Berlin. He earned a Ph.D. from Harvard and wrote brilliant pioneering studies in sociology on race relations and problems. He moved to

Atlanta in 1897. The two African-American leaders clashed over this. For DuBois, only limitless opportunity was acceptable, but Washington said he was content with slow progress.

Chapter 48 — Using Verbs

Exercise A   48a–b Understanding Verb Forms and Tense

The following passage contains choices for the forms of irregular verbs and the tenses of both regular and irregular verbs. Underline the correct choice; the first sentence has been completed as an example.

Many times in history, artwork (represents, <u>has represented</u>) the experience of teaching and learning in various cultures. One of the most famous frescoes to portray education is the School of Athens by Raphael. The work (is located, was located) in one of the Vatican museums. Plato, Aristotle, Socrates, Euclid, Pythagoras, and Ptolemy (are shown, are showed) in the work, surrounded by students. Alexander the Great (brought, brung) Plato's ideas to his conquered lands. An illustration called "The Romance of Alexander the Great," which (hangs, hung) in the Freer Gallery of Art of the Smithsonian Institution, (illustrates, illustrated) Alexander's education. A mosaic in the James Harmon Hoose Library of Philosophy at the University of Southern California (honors, honored) the wisdom of Confucius with a quote on truth (written, wrote) in both Chinese and English.

Additional works of art celebrating education and learning (concentrate, concentrated) on the important discoveries in astronomy and geography. A seventeenth-century painting by Jan Vermeer (shows, has shown) a scholar holding a compass and studying a map. A globe (rests, rested) on a tall cabinet. Astronomers (gather, gathered) around an astrolabe in an early Muslim painting. The Muslim advances in astronomy and geometry (led, lead) to their improved star maps and measure of latitude. Another work shows Galileo demonstrating the telescope to the Senate of Venice.

Galileo (developed, has developed) a telescope powerful enough to discover four satellites of Jupiter.

Source: These works of art were all cited in an article called "Visions of Wisdom," *American Educator* (the magazine of the American Federation of Teachers), Fall 2002, 24–29.

Name _____ Date _____ Score _____

Chapter 48 | Using Verbs

Exercise B   48c Understanding Mood

The following sentences require the subjunctive mood. Underline the correct verb choice.

1. I wish I (was, were) able to hop on a plane and fly to London for the weekend.

2. If I (was, were) to take the advice of my November issue of *In Britain* magazine, I must see a production at the Shakespeare's Globe Theatre.

3. The magazine also advises taking afternoon tea at one of London's top hotels, but I wish I (was, were) back at Harrods for tea and their remarkable tiramisu.

4. If she (was, were) to travel with me, my granddaughter would probably prefer to shop at Harrods, but I would rather tour Hampton Court or Buckingham Palace.

5. The magazine also recommends a tour of Parliament or a ride on the London Eye, but I would prefer that I (was, were) wandering the National Gallery or the Tate before an evening at the theatre.

Chapter 48 | Using Verbs

Exercise C | 48d Understanding Voice

The following passage contains several sentences written in passive voice. Change all passive sentences to active sentences. Are any of the sentences more emphatic in the passive form? How is the emphasis different in the passive and active forms of each sentence?

A system of education designed to teach polite accomplishments was the traditional Japanese *iemoto* system. Skills to be learned by students included flower arrangement, Japanese dance, the tea ceremony, and calligraphy. Monthly fees were paid by beginners, but they could teach and charge fees once they became proficient. The arts and skills learned in the *iemoto* system may be seen as hobbies more than occupational skills.

Another type of early Japanese education was the *terakoya*, or small-scale school. These schools for local children were originally run by temple priests. Minimal reading, writing, and abacus use necessary for everyday life were taught.

Japanese education overall emphasizes collaboration or shared learning. Active participation in meetings, conferences, and groups is expected. A common expression is that "The teacher is often taught." Learning is desired in both formal education and amusement or hobbies. The pleasure is in the learning.

_____

_____

_____

_____

_____

Chapter 49 — Revising Agreement Errors

Exercise A   49a Making Subjects and Verbs Agree

Underline the correct singular or plural verbs in the following passage.

Almost everyone who has studied American history (knows, know) the story of the quest for religious freedom of the Pilgrims who journeyed on the *Mayflower*. However, not as many (study, studies) another group who (was, were) early settlers, the Quakers. This group of religious "seekers" (was founded, were founded) in 1652; a man named George Fox is considered the founder. A small congregation (was formed, were formed) in England and met at the home of Judge Fell and his wife Margaret.

A few Quakers traveled to the New World, but these people (was, were) not tolerated by the Puritans of Massachusetts because Quakers did not accept the Calvinist doctrines of predestination and election. Quakers believed in an "inner light," which seemed to discount authority in the eyes of the Puritans. However, eventually the Quakers found places to settle and practice their beliefs in peace. Several great leaders, among them William Penn and John Woolman, emerged among the Quakers.

While some (recognizes, recognize) the name of William Penn in connection with the state of Pennsylvania, the accomplishments of the early abolitionist and humanitarian John Woolman (are known, is known) to few. Neither Penn nor Woolman (was, were) a religious leader first; each (is, are) more readily identified for other contributions. Besides being the founder of Pennsylvania, Penn is noted for making peace with the Delaware. The Delaware (was, were) a tribe of Native Americans. Among Woolman's accomplishments as a peacemaker and abolitionist (was, were) his antislavery work, *Some Considerations on the Keeping of Negroes.*

Chapter 49 — Revising Agreement Errors

Exercise B   49b Making Pronouns and Antecedents Agree

Underline the correct pronoun in the parentheses. Identify its antecedent with an arrow from the pronoun to the antecedent.

Two other important American Quakers and activists for human rights were Susan B. Anthony and Lucretia Mott. (They, She) fought for women's suffrage or the right of women to vote. Mott and Anthony, along with Elizabeth Cady Stanton, pursued women's suffrage, but each had (her, their) priorities regarding the vote for emancipated slaves, temperance, and (her, their) degree of activism. Mott was a Quaker minister and abolitionist first, but she and Stanton organized the first women's rights convention in the United States at Seneca Falls, New York, in 1848. Stanton and Anthony met in Seneca Falls in 1851; thereafter (she, they) worked together on women's suffrage.

None of these women had (her, their) opportunity to vote because none of them lived to see the Nineteenth Amendment become law in 1920. A statue of Anthony, Mott, and Stanton commemorating (her, their) role in achieving women's suffrage stands in the U.S. Capitol. Anthony was also recognized when one-dollar coins were issued with her image on (it, them).

Chapter 50	**Using Adjectives and Adverbs**

Exercise A	**50a–c Understanding and Using Adjectives and Adverbs**

Underline the correct adjective or adverb in parentheses.

A fascinating variety of rural houses can be found in the Puglia region of Italy. These little houses are called *trulli*. The houses look (strange, strangely) to a visitor because they are circular, with cone-shaped roofs of overlapping stones. The easiest way to experience these houses (quick, quickly) is to travel to the village of Alberobello, located (close, closely) to the cities of Bari and Brindisi. More than one thousand *trulli* are (beautifully, beautiful) nestled here. *Trulli* with multiple rooms consist of multiple cylinders with individual conical roofs. The rooms are joined (smooth, smoothly) with little stone halls, and the exteriors are plastered and whitewashed (careful, carefully). The roofs remain (natural, naturally) stone, and each bears a symbol of the family's identity.

Name _____ Date _____ Score _____

Chapter 50 — Using Adjectives and Adverbs

Exercise B   50d Using Comparative and Superlative Forms

Using the paragraph from the preceding exercise, which has been slightly modified below, change each underlined adjective or adverb to a comparative or superlative form.

A fascinating variety of rural houses may be found in the Puglia region of Italy. These little houses are called *trulli*. These houses look strange to a visitor because they are circular, with cone-shaped roofs of overlapping stones. A quick and easy way to experience these houses is to travel to the village of Alberobello, located close to the cities of Bari and Brindisi. More than one thousand beautiful *trulli* are nestled here. *Trulli* with multiple rooms consist of multiple cylinders with individual conical roofs. The small rooms are joined smoothly with little stone halls, and the exteriors are plastered and whitewashed carefully. The roofs remain natural stone, and each bears a symbol of the family's identity painted in bright white. Some of the symbols are meant to ward off bad luck.

Chapter 51 | Using End Punctuation

Exercise A	51a–c Using Periods, Question Marks, and Exclamation Points

Place the correct end punctuation after each statement.

1. The plight of migratory workers in the United States was greatly improved through the efforts of Cesar Chavez

2. Who was this man of humble origins

3. Chavez had been born in Arizona on the large farm of his grand-parents

4. In the 1930s, the Great Depression and a severe drought forced the Chavez family to give up their ranch

5. What were they to do

6. The family moved to California and became migratory workers

7. They picked fruits and vegetables for low wages and suffered because of terrible working conditions

8. Could Cesar get any type of education

9. He managed to complete eighth grade after attending more than thirty elementary schools

10. Eventually, he joined the Community Service Organization, which urged Mexican Americans to register and vote

11. Later, Chavez organized the National Farm Workers Association, renamed the United Farm Workers (UFW)

12. A strike of California grape-pickers led to a national boycott of table grapes

13. The UFW even received the attention and total support of Robert F. Kennedy

14. Although the Teamsters tried to take power from the UFW, the UFW retains the sole right to organize farm laborers

15. Tragically, Chavez died in 1993 at the age of sixty-six

Chapter 51   Using End Punctuation

Exercise B   **51a–c Using Periods, Question Marks, and Exclamation Points**

Place the correct end punctuation after each statement.

1. Do you know who wrote *The World is Flat: A Brief History of the Twenty-First Century*

2. I'm fascinated by the choice of "flatteners" that Milton Friedman has identified

3. Do you know the significance of the date 11/9/89

4. The second date and "flattener" is 8/9/95

5. The first date is the initial breach of the Berlin Wall, and the second is the public offering of Netscape

6. From 1991 to 1996, the number of Internet users jumped from 600,000 to 40 million

7. Netscape was open source, a universal way to access the Internet

8. I understood Friedman's fourth "flattener" very personally when I had to call the Gateway 800 number late one night

9. Where do you think my service person was based

10. Bangalore

Chapter 52 | Using Commas

Exercise A   52a Setting Off Independent Clauses

Use commas to set off the independent clauses in the following sentences.

EXAMPLE: Frida Kahlo is known as the wife of the great muralist Diego Rivera͵but she was also a great artist in her own right.

1. Kahlo was a young, energetic girl of sixteen when her life was interrupted by a devastating bus accident so she was forced to convalesce in bed for a long while.

2. Her love of painting could not be stopped and she found ways to paint while she was recovering.

3. Soon afterward, she showed her work to the well-known artist Diego Rivera and he encouraged her to continue painting.

4. He believed in her talents and he also fell in love with her.

5. They were married in 1929 when she was nineteen and he was forty-three but their marriage was stormy because he was constantly unfaithful.

6. Kahlo lived in constant pain for the accident had left her with much internal damage and many broken bones.

7. Many of Kahlo's paintings were self-portraits but they include surrealistic details like a bleeding heart, sections of veins, and wounded animals.

8. Her distinctive face is characterized by her single, dark eyebrow and her black hair is often decorated with vivid tropical flowers.

9. Her art was displayed at shows in Mexico and New York City and she may have been the first woman to sell a painting to the Louvre.

10. The American actor, Edward G. Robinson bought some of her paintings but Kahlo did not believe her talents were equal to her famous husband's.

Chapter 52 Using Commas

Exercise B 52b Setting Off Items in a Series

Separate items in a series with commas.

EXAMPLE: Both Frida Kahlo and her husband, Diego Rivera, were artists,
political activists,and friends of Leon Trotsky.

1. Rivera painted huge murals depicting Mexican peasants factory workers and the occasional famous political figure.

2. Kahlo painted smaller self-portraits with bright glossy colors and lush vivid flowers.

3. While many of her images are warmly tropical, details such as a bleeding heart her wounded and broken body and twisted limbs are also featured.

4. Rivera's huge murals are a celebration of the political social industrial and scientific possibilities of the world around him.

5. Henry Ford commissioned Rivera to paint a mural at the Detroit Institute of Arts which celebrates labor industry and the U.S. autoworker.

6. The Rockefellers commissioned a mural called *Man at the Crossroads* for the RCA building in Rockefeller Center, and Rivera chose to portray a clear easily identified picture of Lenin leading a May Day demonstration.

203

7. The patrons who commissioned the mural were so incensed that Rivera was ordered to stop he was paid for his work and the mural was destroyed.

Chapter 52	**Using Commas**

Exercise C   **52c Setting Off Introductory Elements**

Place commas wherever needed to set off introductory elements.

EXAMPLE: Born in Mexico in 1886͵Diego Rivera is one of the greatest artists
of the twentieth century.

1. In 1892 Rivera and his family moved to Mexico City.

2. At the San Carlos Academy he studied art.

3. In 1907 he moved to Europe, and for the next fourteen years he
   studied in Paris.

4. Inspired by the art of Cezanne, Gauguin, Renoir, and Matisse
   Rivera sought his artistic medium.

5. In Italy Rivera studied the Renaissance frescoes.

6. Painted in fresh plaster frescoes provide a medium for large
   works of art on public buildings, which appealed to Rivera's political motives.

7. Because of his interest in Marxism Rivera wanted to reach the
   common people with his art.

8. Throughout the 1920s Rivera painted murals portraying Mexican history.

9. After receiving commissions from the American Stock Exchange Luncheon Club and the California School of the Fine Arts Rivera firmly established his reputation in North America.

10. Capturing the essential parts of a complex subject Rivera continued to portray the history of the working class.

Chapter 52 | Using Commas

Exercise D   52d Setting Off Nonessential Material

Set off nonessential material (nonrestrictive modifiers) in the following sentences. The sentences include a mixture of adjective clauses, prepositional phrases, verbal phrases, and appositives. Introductory elements and series are also included in this exercise.

EXAMPLE: Tina Gulotta, Frank Romero, Margaret Garcia, and Magu‚ a group of Los Angeles artists‚ recently opened a show entitled *Paper,* "Frida on‚ ~~Paper~~" which is inspired by the work of Frida Kahlo.

In 1987 an exhibit of Frida Kahlo's art was brought to the Plaza de la Raza a site in East Los Angeles. The exhibit among the most extensive in the United States at that time drew the attention of Tina Gulotta a young artist. Fifteen years later in 2002 Gulotta was invited to exhibit with other established artists including Frank Romero Margaret Garcia and Magu. The art which explored the many ways Frida Kahlo influenced these artists was prepared specifically for the exhibit. The exhibit anticipating the movie *Frida* opened in October 2002. The movie directed by Julie Taymor opened in November 2002.

Chapter 52 Using Commas

Exercise E 52e Using Commas in Other Conventional Contexts and Comma Review

Insert commas as needed for a variety of conventional contexts, such as addresses, dates, tagging direct quotations, titles, and long numbers. Commas need to be added to the direct quotation as well. Introductory elements, nonessential material, compound sentences, and series also require commas.

According to Diego Rivera "An artist is above all a human being profoundly human to the core. If the artist can't feel everything that humanity feels if the artist isn't capable of loving until he forgets himself and sacrifices himself if necessary if he won't put down his magic brush and head the fight against the oppressor then he isn't a great artist."

Born in Guanajuato Mexico in 1886 Diego Rivera spent a lifetime committed to the struggles of workers both in Mexico and internationally. Although he and his wife Frida Kahlo noted Mexican artist were controversial for their Communist sympathies they both acquired an international reputation for their great art. In the United States Rivera's murals can be seen in Detroit New York and California. Specifically important murals on the West Coast can be seen at the California Palace of the Legion of Honor San Francisco California and the California School of the Fine Arts University of Southern California.

Source of quotation: *American Masters*. Public Broadcasting System. 28 May 2004 <http://www.pbs.org/wnet/americanmasters/database/rivera_d.html>

Chapter 53   Using Semicolons

Exercise A   53a–c Separating Independent Clauses and Items in a Series

Combine these short sentences by inserting semicolons to separate independent clauses or to create complex series.

EXAMPLE: Mount Vesuvius, located near Naples, Italy, violently erupted in
A.D. 79. The city of Pompeii was completely destroyed.
; the (inserted above, replacing ". The")

1. Evidence of a small settlement in Pompeii dates back to the ninth century BC. However, the city destroyed by Mount Vesuvius was a thriving metropolis.

2. An Etruscan community had settled at the site between the fifth and sixth centuries BC. Evidence includes their earlier structures under the Temple of Apollo, located near the entrance to the ruins. Additional evidence includes the Stabian baths. More evidence occurs under the Triangular Forum.

3. Greek colonies followed the Etruscans in the Campania region of Italy. This region includes ancient Pompeii and the modern city of Naples.

4. By the second century BC, Pompeii was a thriving, prosperous city. However, war came when the Romans invaded in 80 BC.

5. Clear signs of the Romanization of Pompeii include several structures. One building is the Capitolium, dedicated to Jupiter, Juno, and Minerva. Another structure is the Temple of Venus. A third structure is the Forum Baths, built behind the Capitolium.

6. After 20 BC, the preferences of Augustus Caesar and other emperors were imposed on Pompeii. These preferences included worship of specific deities such as Venus, which led to the rebuilding of the Temple of Venus. Another preference was the worship of the emperor himself, which resulted in the building of the Temple of Vespasian. Worship of gods of the town led to the Temple of the Public Lares.

7. The final day of this thriving city was August 24 in AD 79. Until then, Mt. Vesuvius was a beautifully green mountain.

8. A description of the eruption survives from Pliny the Younger, Admiral of the Roman Fleet stationed at Miseno. His uncle, Pliny the Elder, was found dead on the beach of Stabiae.

9. The eruption started with the deafening noise of the rupture of solidified lava sealing the volcano's summit. The next step was a shower of pumice stone, falling to a depth of two and a half meters. The third step was a thick layer of volcanic ash, which fell for four days.

10. More than 10,000 inhabitants died. Causes of death were the poisonous gases from the pumice stones and suffocation from the ash.

Chapter 53	**Using Semicolons**

Exercise B   **53d Editing Misused Semicolons**

Edit for misused semicolons; replace semicolons with appropriate punctuation.

Pliny the Younger wrote of his experience witnessing the eruption of Mt. Vesuvius; and the destruction of Pompeii. He watched from Stabia; where his friend Pomponianus had a villa. Pliny states the following in a letter to the historian Tacitus; "[. . .] people were afraid of the shower of lapilli stones falling outside." He added that his host "chose to go outside . . . he put some pillows on his head and secured them with sheets."

The few survivors began excavations; seeking to locate their statues and sacred objects from the ruins of their homes. However, the site remained barren and former inhabitants settled elsewhere; abandoning the desolate place forever. Not until centuries later did archaeologists begin successful excavation of the site.

Source of quotation and information: *The Guide to the Archaeological Site Pompeii*, in English from Marius Edizioni, *Pompeii*, 2002.

Chapter 54 | Using Apostrophes

Exercise A | 54a Forming the Possessive Case

Change the word or phrase in parentheses to its possessive form.

EXAMPLE: (~~Shah Jehan~~) *Shah Jehan's* great love for his wife, Mumtaz Mahal, led him to build the beautiful Taj Mahal after her death in 1630.

1. Shah (Jehan) marriage to Mumtaz Mahal was the (emperor) second marriage, but it was a true love match.

2. Mumtaz Mahal was her (husband) constant companion and advisor, and she inspired him to kindness for the needy.

3. The (empress) death during childbirth left the emperor grief-stricken.

4. As a testament to their deep love, Shah Jehan had one of the (world) most beautiful buildings constructed as her mausoleum.

5. (Mumtaz Mahal) tomb is part of a complex including a mosque and beautiful gardens.

6. The vast (complex) structure includes outer walls to enclose it completely and a main gateway.

7. Twenty-two (years) labor combining twenty thousand (workmen) efforts was needed to complete the complex, finished in 1648.

Chapter 54	**Using Apostrophes**

Exercise B	**54b–d Indicating Omissions in Contractions, Forming Plurals, and Editing Misused Apostrophes**

In the following passage, underline the correct form for possessive nouns, contractions, plurals, possessive pronouns, and numbers provided in the parentheses.

No one knows the exact origin of the name "Taj Mahal," but (its, it's) usually translated to mean "Crown of the Palace." (Its, It's) the mausoleum and complex for Mumtaz Mahal (whose, who's) marriage to Shah Jehan in 1612 was the start of one of the great love (stories, story's) of all time. In the (1600s, 1600's), India was ruled by mughal monarchs, and Shah Jehan was one of them. He went on many journeys and military expeditions accompanied by his beloved wife, who eventually died giving birth.

The (Taj Mahals, Taj Mahal's) location is Agra, India, on the banks of the Yamuna River. The (Yamuna Rivers, Yamuna River's) source is the Himalaya Mountains, and the Yamuna then flows eastward into the Ganges River. The (complexes, complex's) buildings, gardens, and a reflecting pond are designed for serenity and harmony. A mosque and prayer house enhance the (tomb's, tombs) contemplative atmosphere.

Chapter 55 Using Quotation Marks

Exercise A   55a Setting Off Quoted Speech or Writing

Add quotation marks where necessary to set off quotations from identifying tags.

1. Most people remember W. C. Fields saying Never give a sucker an even break.

2. Another of Fields's curmudgeonly sayings was Anyone who hates children and dogs can't be all bad.

3. Fields's notorious drinking led to statements like 'Twas a woman who drove me to drink, which he concluded with, and I never had the courtesy to thank her for it.

4. I like children. If they're properly cooked, stated Fields.

5. I am free of all prejudices, Fields commented. I hate everyone equally.

6. Fields's political leanings are encapsulated in this quotation: I never voted *for* anyone. I always voted against.

Source of quotations: "Fields, W. C." *Uncle John's Second Bathroom Reader*. The Bathroom Reader's Institute. New York: St. Martin's Press, 1989. 29.

Chapter 55   Using Quotation Marks

Exercise B   55c Setting Off Titles

The titles in the following passage have all been placed in italics. Use quotation marks instead for titles of appropriate works. Some titles will remain in italics.

One of the most productive and controversial African-American writers of the twentieth century was James Baldwin. His most well-known novel is probably *Go Tell It on the Mountain* (1952), but his collection of short stories called *Going to Meet the Man* (1965) includes the title short story, *Going to Meet the Man*, a tale of brutal racial violence in the Deep South. The frequently anthologized and popular story, *Sonny's Blues*, appears in the same collection.

Baldwin also published several collections of essays and two plays, *Blues for Mister Charlie* and *Amen Corner*. His powerful critique of racism in Harriet Beecher Stowe's *Uncle Tom's Cabin*, entitled *Everybody's Favorite Protest Novel*, defined the concept of the "Uncle Tom" as one who betrays his own race.

Chapter 55 | Using Quotation Marks

Exercise C | 55e Using Quotation Marks with Other Punctuation

Place quotation marks as needed. Be sure to place them correctly when in combination with other punctuation. Also note that one quotation is within a quotation and make changes if italics are used incorrectly.

In his essay entitled Remembering Richard Wright, Ralph Ellison recalls his fellow African-American writer. Ellison begins with a meditation on Heraclitus' axiom, Geography is fate. Ellison grew up in Oklahoma, while Richard Wright was born in Mississippi and moved to Chicago. Ellison observes, Thus, while we both grew up in segregated societies, mine lacked many of the intensities of custom, tradition, and manners which "colored" institutions of the Old South, and which were important in shaping Wright's point of view.

The men met in New York in 1937, and Ellison indicates that he recognized Wright's potential in a poem published in the *New Masses*. He is also thankful that Langston Hughes was responsible for introducing the two men and for sharing two novels, Malraux's *Man's Fate* and *The Days of Wrath*. Ellison was able to read the manuscript of Wright's *Native Son* as it came from the typewriter. Ellison admired Wright's passion and desire to be recognized, as Ellison states, in terms of his talent, and not in terms of his race or his Mississippi upbringing.

Source of quotations: Young, Al, and Ishmael Reed, Eds. *African-American Literature: A Brief Introduction and Anthology*. Boston, Addison-Wesley Literary Mosaic Series, 1997.

Name _____ Date _____ Score _____

Place colons where needed in the following sentences.

EXAMPLE: The following are my favorite Christmas carols : "Silent Night," "We Three Kings," and "The Holly and the Ivy."

1. The second through fourth verses of "We Three Kings" are the words of the three Wise Men Gaspar, Balthazar, and Melchior.

2. The legendary names of the three Wise Men are Gaspar, Balthazar, and Melchior.

3. They explain the meanings of their three gifts of gold, myrrh, and frankincense.

4. The Wise Men brought the following three gifts gold, myrrh, and frankincense.

5. "The Holly and the Ivy" explains the symbolism of the Christmas colors red and green.

6. Franz Gruber's gentle carol, "Silent Night," begins with the following words "Silent Night, Holy Night, all is calm, all is bright."

7. Franz Gruber's gentle carol, "Silent Night," begins with "Silent Night, Holy Night, all is calm, all is bright."

Chapter 56 | Using Other Punctuation Marks

Exercise B | 56b–e Using Dashes, Parentheses, Brackets, and Slashes

Insert the following punctuation in the paragraph below:

- A slash to indicate lines of poetry
- Parentheses for documentation
- Parentheses for a nonessential date
- A dash to introduce a summarizing statement
- Two dashes to set off nonessential material and create emphasis

One of William Shakespeare's most noteworthy villains is Iago, the adversary to Othello in *The Tragedy of Othello, the Moor of Venice* 1603–4. Iago's motivation is clear fierce jealousy over the promotion of Cassio to the position of lieutenant. Iago will exploit Othello's trusting nature, as he states: "The Moor is of a free and open nature, That thinks men honest that but seem to be so" 1.3.381–2.

Inciting lust in Roderigo, luring Cassio into drunkenness, verbally insulting his wife Emilia Iago exploits the weaknesses and desires of many characters. Ultimately, he arouses jealousy in Othello and incites him to murder his innocent and beloved wife Desdemona.

Chapter 56 | Using Other Punctuation Marks

Exercise C | 56f Using Ellipses

The following is a prose passage spoken by Iago to Roderigo in Shakespeare's *The Tragedy of Othello, the Moor of Venice*. Delete the material indicated in bold print, and use ellipses correctly to indicate the deletions.

IAGO: It is merely a lust of the blood and a permission of the will. Come, be a man. **Drown thyself? Drown cats and blind puppies.** I have professed me thy friend, **and I confess me knit to thy deserving with cables of perdurable toughness.** I could never better stead thee than now. Put money in thy purse. Follow thou the wars, **defeat they favour with an usurped beard. I say,** put money in thy purse. It cannot be long that Desdemona should continue her love to the Moor—**put money in thy purse—**nor he his to her (1.3.329–37).

Chapter 57 | Capitalization

Exercise A | 57b Capitalizing Proper Nouns

The following passage includes an assortment of proper nouns; capitalize all of them.

In the summer of 1911, hiram bingham stumbled upon the incan settlement we now know as machu picchu. Bingham was a yale university archaeologist, the governor of connecticut, a u.s. senator, and a likely model for the hollywood character, indiana jones.

Bingham believed this remote site in the peruvian mountains was a sacred site, a place for worshipping the god of the sun. However, current archaeologists question bingham's interpretation. Some claim it was a pleasure site or retreat for emperor pachacuti in the fifteenth century. The court could escape from the commotion at the capital, cuzco. Two current yale archaeologists, richard burger and his wife lucy salazar, have reinterpreted the artifacts. More than four hundred incan artifacts from machu picchu are currently on tour throughout the united states.

Chapter 57 — Knowing When to Capitalize

Exercise B — 57f Editing Misused Capitals

The following passage uses excessive capitalization. Change unnecessary capitals to lower case.

During the Debutante Season each February in Laredo, Texas, young women attend the Costume Ball for the Society of Martha Washington. Young women dressed in lavish period costumes of Beaded Satin and Velvet, which often cost around $30,000, reenact the lives of George and Martha Washington. A narrator presents a Bilingual story of the Washingtons, in Spanish and in English.

Laredo is a border city between Texas and Mexico, with the International Bridge spanning the Rio Grande River. The City was founded in 1755 under the rule of Spain on both sides of the River. The United States defeated Mexico in 1948, and Laredo on the Texas side became part of the Union. The town has a history of a distinct Class Structure, with wealthy citizens prospering from Commerce, Oil, and Gas. Celebration of Washington's Birthday began during the Spanish-American War in 1898 to show Patriotism to the United States, and the Martha Washington Society was added in 1939.

Chapter 58   Italics

Exercise A   58a–c Setting Off Titles, Names, Foreign Words, Phrases, Elements Spoken of as Themselves, and Terms Being Defined

Underline all titles, names of specific works, foreign words and phrases, elements spoken of as themselves, and terms being defined that would require italics in a printed work.

EXAMPLE: In Sophocles' famous Greek tragedy, <u>Oedipus Rex</u>, Oedipus suffers from the tragic flaw of <u>hubris</u> or pride.

1. Sophocles actually wrote a trilogy, called The Theban Cycle, which included Oedipus Rex, Oedipus at Colonus, and Antigone.

2. Although Sophocles only won second place for Oedipus Rex, the play's place in history was assured in Aristotle's Poetics.

3. Aristotle saw the traits of Sophocles' play as defining tragedy.

4. A tragic hero needed a flaw, or hamartia, such as the hubris Oedipus exhibited.

5. Aristotle identified two tragic emotions, fear and pity, which would lead the audience to a catharsis, an emotional release.

6. Later writers, such as the Roman writer Horace, in his The Art of Poetry, saw Aristotle's analysis as more of a set of rules.

7. Translating Aristotle's Greek into other languages led to some shifting of meaning, such as Lodovico Castelvetro's use of the Italian imitazione for Aristotle's word mimesis in Castelvetro's work On Aristotle's Poetics.

Chapter 58 | Using Italics

| Exercise B | 58a–c Setting Off Titles, Names, Foreign Words, Phrases, Elements Spoken of as Themselves, and Terms Being Defined |

Underline all titles, names of specific works, foreign words and phrases, elements spoken of as themselves, and terms being defined that would require italics in a printed work.

Khaled Hosseini's novel, The Kite Runner, published in 2003 became a #1 New York Times bestseller. The novel is a story of tragedy and transformation set in Afghanistan before and during its occupation by the Russians and the Taliban. The character named Amir grows up with Hassan, the Hazzara boy that Amir's father sired after the death of Amir's mother. The boys grow up together, eating simple foods like kofta and naan. Amir, the legitimate son, studied Islam under a mullah, learning of zakat, the duty of hadj, and the five daily namaz prayers. Hassan did not attend school and remained illiterate until adulthood.

In Afghanistan before the occupation, a favorite sport was kite tournaments, with young boys flying kites attached to glass-covered strings. They would compete to cut down each other's kites, and the kite runners would chase the untethered kites as prizes. Hassan was famous as the best of kite runners.

Once the Russians and then the Taliban conquered the homeland or watan, Amir's and Hassan's lives were changed forever. Amir and his father escaped to America, Hassan was killed by the Taliban, and eventually Amir returned to Kabul to rescue Hassan's orphaned son and take him to America.

Chapter 59	Hyphens

Exercise A	59b Dividing Compound Words

Insert hyphens as needed to create correct compound words.

EXAMPLE: With the rapid increase in home-improvement retail stores,
do-it-yourself
everyone can be a ~~do it yourself~~ genius with minimal effort.

1. The days of brick and board bookshelves are a thing of the past now that simple, pre cut kits are readily available.

2. For under $30, smaller kits with attractive wood tone finishes and pre drilled sections can be purchased at most discount and home improvement stores.

3. Some kits require a few personal hand tools, such as a flat or Phillips head screwdriver, but others come complete with little Allen wrenches.

4. Step by step directions are enclosed, usually in both English and Spanish versions.

5. Illustrations to accompany the directions provide much needed visual support.

6. Smaller kits are lightweight and portable, but larger projects are heavy and might require assistance in assembling.

7. Half inch particle board shelves are usually sturdy enough to hold small books and paperbacks.

8. Overly heavy books may cause shelves to sag over time and require a heavy duty unit.

Chapter 59 | Using Hyphens

Exercise B | **59b Dividing Compound Words**

Insert hyphens as needed to create correct compound words.

1. The skeleton of a three year old child called the Dikika baby was found in Ethiopia in 2000.

2. Her 3.3 million year old bones predate the famous skeleton of Lucy, a 3.2 million year old adult.

3. Foreign led expeditions have dominated research in the past, but a paleoanthropologist named Zeresenay led the Ethiopian team that found Dikika baby.

4. The skeleton includes a pea sized kneecap.

5. Dikika baby's upper body has many ape like features.

6. Her brain volume was similar to a three year old chimp's and much smaller than a human's.

Chapter 60 | Abbreviations

Exercise A | 60a–d Abbreviating and Editing Misused Abbreviations

Revise incorrectly used abbreviations in the following sentences. Some abbreviations may be acceptable.

EXAMPLE: A ~~no.~~ *number* of animals have become famous stars in their own right.

1. One of the most famous animal actors was Lassie, who starred in seven feature films and a series that ran for nineteen yrs.

2. Lassie was created in 1938 by a writer named Eric Knight, but he sold his rights to MGM in 1941 and received no royalties.

3. Smokey the Bear was named after "Smokey Joe" Martin, Asst. Fire Chief of N.Y.C. between 1919 and 1930.

4. The U.S. government employs secretaries to answer Smokey's mail.

5. Elsie the Cow appeared as a cartoon on Borden products, but they selected a 975 lb. Jersey to appear in the 1939 New York World's Fair as Elsie.

6. Morris the Cat was rescued from an animal shelter in Hinsdale, Ill., to become the famous cat-food representative.

7. Hollywood trainer Carl Spitz owned the dog who became famous as Toto in *The Wizard of Oz*, starring J. Garland as Dorothy.

Source of information: "You Animal!" *Uncle John's Second Bathroom Reader*. The Bathroom Reader's Institute. New York: St. Martin's, 1989. 51–52 .

Chapter 60 | Using Abbreviations

Exercise B | 60a–d Abbreviating and Editing Misused Abbreviations

Revise incorrectly used abbreviations in the following paragraph. Some abbreviations may be acceptable.

Most of us are familiar with a famous address: 1600 Pennsylvania Ave. Actually, the full address is 1600 Penn. Ave. NW, Washington D.C. 20500. If we go to the Web site at www.whitehouse.gov, we can learn about the history of the building and its famous occupants. In addition, people planning a trip to D.C. may call the 24-hour Visitors Office Info Line at 202–456–7041.

The portion of the White House that we associate with the work of the President of the U.S. is the West Wing. It consists of four rooms: the Cabinet Rm., the Oval Office, the Press Rm., and the Roosevelt Rm. The Oval Office was built in 1909, and Pres. W.H. Taft was the first president to use it. The Roosevelt Room was the presidential office before 1909. Richard Nixon named the room for Theodore Roosevelt in 1969. On the mantel is the Nobel Peace Prize won by T. Roosevelt in 1906.

Chapter 61 Numbers

Exercise A **61a–b Spelled-Out Numbers versus Numerals and Conventional Uses of Numerals**

Spell out numbers where necessary. Retain numerals as appropriate.

1. From ages 5 to 15, the average American child will view the killing of about 13,500 people on television.

2. 39% of Americans believe winning the lottery is the best way to get rich.

3. A car could drive around the world 4 times with the amount of fuel held in a jumbo jet.

4. In the 1980s, 60 percent of all new cars sold were recalled for some defect.

5. Only 2 people, John Hancock and Charles Thomson, signed the Declaration of Independence on July 4, 1776.

6. Before 1863, mail service in the United States was free.

7. Yuri Gagarin, the Russian astronaut, was 27 when he orbited the earth on April 12, 1961.

8. In 1964, a McDonald's hamburger cost $0.15.

9. 3–5 gallons of water go down the drain in 1 minute from a running faucet.

10. "96 Tears" was a hit song of the 1960s.

Source of information: *Uncle John's Second Bathroom Reader*. The Bathroom Reader's Institute. New York: St. Martin's, 1989.

Chapter 61 | Using Numbers

Exercise B | 61a–b Spelled-Out Numbers versus Numerals and Conventional Uses of Numerals

Spell out numbers where necessary. Retain numerals as appropriate.

On 3/6/1836, the famous Siege and Battle of the Alamo took place. Once named the Mision San Antonio de Valero, the site we now call The Alamo was first constructed in 1724. The complex sits on a little over 4 acres and is now owned by the State of Texas. The Daughters of the Republic of Texas maintain it.

The famous battle took place between the Mexican attackers led by Santa Anna and the defenders, known as "Texians." Exact figures are not known for the death toll, but the number of Texians, including 32 members of the Gonzales Ranging Company, is now set at 189. 9 Tejanos, or Hispanic Texans, are identified as killed. The estimated number of Mexican soldiers who died is 521. The Web site for the Alamo lists 12 survivors and mentions that 2 captured doctors were spared because they were needed to treat the wounded in San Antonio.

Chapter 63 | Grammar and Style for ESL Writers

Exercise A   63a Solving Verb-Related Problems

The following paragraphs have several verb errors, which have been under-lined. Look for the following types of mistake and correct them; then, label each type of error.

- Subject-verb agreement
- Tense shifts
- Participle forms
- Placement in the sentence

Each January, Americans <u>are celebrating</u> Martin Luther King Day. King <u>was</u> the only American besides George Washington to have a national holiday designated for his birthday. For fifteen years, from King's death in 1968 to legislation in 1983, people lobbied for the holiday to honor King. Petitions with more than six million signa-tures <u>were being presented</u> to Congress.

Why it <u>was</u> so hard to make King's birthday a national holiday? Some people, such as former Senator Jesse Helms of North Carolina, <u>were thinking</u> King was a Communist or a troublemaker. Others <u>say</u> the cost of lost wages for a day off would be very high. Opponents <u>were saying</u> the day off would cost $8 billion. Still others <u>were saying</u> King was not so special and that other famous people <u>was</u> more important.

Martin Luther King Day is not exactly a patriotic holiday like most U.S. national holidays. However, it is a good day to honor Dr. King's beliefs. He <u>wants</u> us to respect and love our fellow human beings.

| Chapter 63 | **Grammar and Style for ESL Writers** |

Exercise B   63b Solving Noun-Related Problems

The following paragraphs have several noun-related errors, which have been underlined. Look for the following types of mistake and correct them; then, label each type of error.

• Noncount nouns

• Articles with nouns

• Other determiners

The national holiday <u>number two</u> in America each year is George Washington's birthday on February 22. George Washington was <u>first</u> president of <u>United States</u>. Washington was born in <u>colony</u> of Virginia on February 22, 1732, and died in <u>state</u> of Virginia on December 14, 1799.

When Washington was elected Commander in Chief of <u>Continental Army</u> in 1775, the Congress took his <u>advices</u> to be cautious in war. The troops lacked <u>equipments</u> and supplies. After <u>American Revolution</u>, Washington hoped to retire to his beautiful home, <u>the Mount Vernon</u>. However, he came out of <u>the retirement</u> to serve his country when <u>U.S. Constitution</u> was ratified in 1787.

Some states celebrate Abraham Lincoln's birthday on the February 12, and some celebrate Presidents' Day on <u>third Monday</u> of February, but these dates are not <u>the national holidays</u>.

| Chapter 63 | **Grammar and Style for ESL Writers** |

| **Exercise C** | **63c Using Pronouns** |

In the following paragraphs, replace the underlined nouns with pronouns. Be careful of pronoun case, number, and gender.

Although Americans seldom have a day off from work on June 14th, the day was declared National Flag Day in 1949. The celebration probably originated in 1885 in Fredonia, Wisconsin, where a schoolteacher, B. J. Cigrand, wanted to honor the anniversary of the adoption of the Stars and Stripes as the American flag. The flag was adopted on June 14, 1777, by a Flag Resolution, and the flag was finally honored with a celebration at the Betsy Ross House in Philadelphia in 1891. Betsy Ross was the legendary creator of the flag, and Betsy Ross chose the design of red and white stripes, a field of blue, and thirteen white stars.

The city of Philadelphia took the lead in promoting Flag Day. The city of Philadelphia adopted a resolution to display the flag on June 14. By 1893, children of Philadelphia assembled in Independence Square. The children of Philadelphia carried small flags and sang patriotic songs. Organizations in New York and Illinois also supported Flag Day celebrations. In 1894, more than 300,000 Chicago schoolchildren participated in ceremonies in that city's public parks.

President Woodrow Wilson established Flag Day in 1916. President Woodrow Wilson did not, however, create a national holiday. President Harry S. Truman signed an Act of Congress on August 3, 1949. President Truman's signature finalized June 14 as National Flag Day.

Chapter 63 — Grammar and Style for ESL Writers

Exercise D   63c Using Pronouns

Underline all of the pronouns in the following passage. Identify the noun reference for each pronoun.

The most important national holiday for Americans is Independence Day, celebrated on July 4. It commemorates the signing of the Declaration of Independence on July 4, 1776, in Philadelphia, Pennsylvania. This document is a formal argument addressed to the King of England, George III, and the English Parliament. It states all the reasons that the thirteen colonies were compelled to declare their independence. The colonies were reluctant to declare war with England, but they saw no other choice.

Thomas Jefferson was the primary writer of the Declaration. His original draft was very forceful, and he used wording to end the slave trade at the same time. However, the delegates edited and softened his language a bit. A vote to accept the Declaration was taken on July 4. Nine colonies voted in favor of the Declaration, Pennsylvania and South Carolina voted against it, Delaware was undecided, and New York abstained. Actually, several weeks passed before all the signatures were gathered on the document.

Chapter 63   Grammar and Style for ESL Writers

Exercise E   63e Using Prepositions

Underline the correct preposition in the following sentences.

EXAMPLE: (On, <u>In</u>) the month of March, some people celebrate Pulaski Day.

1. Casimir Pulaski was a Polish nobleman who assisted the Americans (in, for) the American Revolution.

2. He was born (on, in) either March 4 or March 6, 1945, (into, in) Poland.

3. Pulaski served as a cavalry commander in the Polish fight (against, toward) the Russians.

4. The Polish forces lost, and Pulaski fled (into, to) Paris, where he (met, met with) Benjamin Franklin.

5. Pulaski received a letter (in, of) recommendation from Franklin and sailed (into, to) America.

6. He reported (onto, to) General George Washington and took part (in, on) his first American battle (in, on) September 11, 1777.

7. Pulaski was (made, made into) general of the American cavalry, later known as the Pulaski Legion.

8. Pulaski was mortally wounded (in, on) an attack (on, in) the city of Savannah.

9. For many years, people believed Pulaski was buried (at, into the) sea.

10. However, his bones were found and identified (in, on) 1996 under the Savannah Pulaski Monument.

Chapter 63 Grammar and Style for ESL Writers

Exercise F   63f Understanding Word Order

Read the following paragraphs for information. Then construct the types of sentences described below the paragraphs and answer the questions.

Memorial Day was officially proclaimed as a tribute to soldiers after the American Civil War. General John Logan issued an order on May 5, 1868, and the first Memorial Day was celebrated on May 30, 1868. The holiday was originally named Decoration Day, and it was meant to honor all who died in the service of the United States. Flowers were placed on the graves of both Union and Confederate soldiers at Arlington National Cemetery for that first commemoration. However, the holiday did not become an officially recognized national holiday until 1948.

Customs for celebrating Memorial Day have changed over the years. In 1915, Moina Michael was the first to wear a red poppy on Memorial Day. She was inspired by the poem "In Flanders Fields," and she wrote a poem in response. The idea of red poppies caught on, and they were soon sold to benefit war orphans. Since the late 1950s, soldiers of the 3rd U.S. Infantry have placed small American flags on the 260,000 gravestones at Arlington National Cemetery. Many other organizations place flags, candles, and other memorials at the gravesites of soldiers throughout the country.

1. Form a question asking when the first Memorial Day was proclaimed.

   Question: _____

   _____

   _____

Answer: _____

_____

_____

2. Form a question asking what the original name of Memorial
   Day was.

   Question: _____

   _____

   _____

   Answer: _____

   _____

   _____

3. Form a question asking how the first Memorial Day was com-
   memorated.

   Question: _____

   _____

   _____

   Answer: _____

   _____

   _____

4. State a command telling someone to name the person who wore
   the first red poppy.

   Question: _____

   _____

   _____

   Answer: _____

   _____

   _____

5. Form a question asking who benefited from the sale of red poppies.

Question: _____

_____

_____

Answer: _____

_____

_____

6. State a command asking someone to name three ways to commemorate Memorial Day.

Question: _____

_____

_____

Answer: _____

_____

_____